THE COMEBACK EDIT

LIFE BEYOND SURVIVAL MODE

TAMMY GIBSON

ISBN: 978-1-971349-21-3

Dedication

For the woman who's ready to stop surviving and start truly living again.
You are stronger, braver, and more capable than you've ever imagined. You are!

Table of Contents

Foreword

By Cotie Williams, Director, PossAbilities

I met Tammy two years ago, shortly after learning about the unimaginable challenges she had faced — losing a limb and her mobility, and enduring countless surgeries as a result of a lengthy hospital stay with complications from COVID-19. From the very beginning, I was struck by her unwavering strength, grace, and determination.

Tammy is the embodiment of resilience. Her steadfast faith, unshakable spirit, and "tough as nails" attitude inspire everyone who has the privilege of knowing her. She faces life not with bitterness, but with purpose — transforming her pain into a powerful message of hope and perseverance.

Beyond her personal journey, Tammy has become a beacon of light and leadership within the amputee and disabled community. As an ambassador and advocate for those newly injured, she offers compassion, guidance, and courage to others finding their way through unimaginable change.

Tammy's journey is not just one of survival, but of transformation. Her words carry the kind of wisdom that can only come from walking through fire and choosing faith over fear. As you turn these pages, I encourage you to open your heart to her story — to the lessons of courage, gratitude, and grace that shine through every chapter. May her strength remind you that even when life changes in ways we never expect, there is always hope, purpose, and a reason to keep moving forward.

It is my honor to introduce you to my friend, Tammy — a living testament to resilience and the power of faith.

Introduction

The room was quiet except for the rhythmic hiss of oxygen filling the hyperbaric chamber.

I could not see much, only the curve of glass, the sterile white ceiling, and a faint reflection of my own face. I was strapped in for another round of treatment to help my wounds heal. It was supposed to bring life back into my body, but instead, I felt trapped inside of it.

Each treatment lasted about an hour, and I remember feeling uneasy every time they closed the chamber door. The anxiety began the moment I was wheeled out of my hospital room. By the time they sealed the chamber, I was already struggling to get comfortable. I kept asking how much longer I had, but I had no sense of time at all. The minutes stretched endlessly, and the whole session felt like it would never end.

During my fifth treatment, I began to seize.

A Code Blue was called. The medical team rushed to my side, but because the chamber was pressurized, they could not open it for several minutes. My body convulsed inside while they waited for the pressure to equalize.

By the time they reached me, I was unresponsive.

I was intubated again, placed on a ventilator, and taken for a brain scan. My family was told to prepare for the possibility that I might not come back as the same woman they knew.

But by the grace of God, I did.

And I did not just return, I came back changed.

Humbled. Healed. Hungry for purpose.

That was the moment my life became more than a recovery story. It became a reclamation.

For months, I had focused on survival, healing, breathing, and enduring. But what I did not realize at the time was that survival is not the finish line. Survival is the starting point for transformation.

Once the storm passed, I had to learn how to live again, physically, emotionally, spiritually. I had to rebuild my confidence, rediscover joy, and redefine what strength really meant. I had to edit my life, not to erase what happened, but to reveal what was still possible.

That is what this book is about.

It is about the space between who you were and who you are becoming.

It is about finding purpose in what is left after everything changes.

And it is about realizing that resilience is not just pushing through the hard parts, it is learning to live fully on the other side of them.

I call it The Comeback Edit.

It is not about pretending everything is fine. It is about telling the truth with faith and courage. It is about taking what life handed you and saying, "This will not define me. It will refine me."

You will read pieces of my journey here, hospital stays, physical therapy, personal reinvention, but this book is not just my story. It is an invitation into yours.

Maybe you are in a season of change, navigating loss, burnout, or transition. Maybe your body, career, or relationships do not look like you thought they would. Maybe you are tired of being strong and ready to feel alive again.

If so, this book is for you.

You will learn how to pause when life demands you to push, how to reflect without shame, how to refine what no longer fits, and how to rebuild with grace and joy.

Through it all, you will see what I discovered, that God's grace does not just meet us in the comeback. It is the reason we can rise at all.

So wherever you find yourself as you turn this first page, take a deep breath.

You are not starting over.

You are starting differently.

And that difference, your perspective, your courage, your story, is exactly what will light the path forward.

Welcome to The Comeback Edit.

Let us begin again, together.

What came next was the moment that would test every truth I believed about strength.

Life Beyond Survival Mode

There is a particular kind of strength that looks impressive on the outside but feels exhausting on the inside.

It's the strength of getting through the day.
Of holding it together.
Of functioning, producing, showing up, and being "fine."

If you're reading this, there's a good chance you've mastered that kind of strength.

You've survived something. Maybe more than one thing. Loss. Illness. Burnout. Disappointment. A season that asked more of you than you thought you had to give. You learned how to endure. You learned how to adapt. You learned how to keep going.

But somewhere along the way, survival became your default setting.

This book begins with a simple but unsettling question:
What if surviving is no longer enough?

Why This Book Exists

We live in a culture that celebrates resilience but rarely teaches restoration. We applaud grit, perseverance, and pushing through, yet we leave little room for integration, reflection, or renewal. The message is often subtle but persistent: *Be strong. Move on. Get back to normal.*

But what if "normal" no longer fits?

What if the version of you that emerged from what you've lived through is asking for something deeper than productivity or praise?

For me, that question wasn't theoretical. It was spiritual.

In the quiet spaces after the crisis, when strength was gone and certainty had dissolved, I discovered that faith is not about having answers. It's about learning how to remain when everything familiar falls away. It's about being held when you can no longer hold yourself.

The Comeback Edit: Life Beyond Survival Mode was written from that space.

Why I'm the One Writing This

I didn't come to this work through theory. I came to it through life itself.

I nearly lost my life. I did lose my leg. And in the long aftermath of trauma, hospitalization, and a body that no longer felt like home, survival became my full-time job.

But survival, I learned, is not the same as healing.

In that season, faith stopped being something I talked about and became something I leaned on. Not in grand declarations, but in quiet dependence. In prayers without words. In learning to trust God when the future felt unrecognizable.

This book is shaped by lived experience, years of walking alongside women navigating profound life transitions, and a deep conviction that God does not waste what we endure. That even in the most disorienting seasons, He is present, attentive, and at work.

What This Book Is (and What It Isn't)

The Comeback Edit is not about bouncing back.
It is not about minimizing pain or rushing redemption.
And it is not about becoming someone new.

It is about **editing what no longer serves you**, honoring what shaped you, and intentionally choosing how you want to live next.

It's about allowing God to meet you in the in-between.
The space after survival.
The place where strength gives way to surrender, and surrender makes room for something truer.

Inside these pages, you'll be invited to examine old narratives, release expectations you were never meant to carry, and reconnect with the parts of yourself that were quieted in the name of getting through.

This is not a checklist. It's a conversation. One rooted in honesty, compassion, and grace.

How the Book Is Structured

Each chapter builds on the last, guiding you through a thoughtful progression:

- Understanding survival mode and how it takes hold
- Naming the hidden costs of always being "strong"
- Creating space for reflection without guilt
- Reclaiming identity after disruption
- Redefining resilience through faith and truth
- Learning how to live with intention, not urgency

Throughout the book, you'll find personal stories, reflection prompts, and moments of pause designed to help you listen. To yourself. To God. To what's quietly asking to be restored.

An Invitation

You don't need to prove anything to be here.
You don't need to justify your exhaustion or your longing for more.
And you don't need to have all the answers.

Faith does not require certainty. It requires willingness.

If you're open to the possibility that God is doing something deeper than you can see, even now, this book is for you.

This is your invitation to edit with care.
To release what kept you alive but no longer lets you thrive.
To trust that what comes next can be shaped with intention and grace.

Turn the page when you're ready.
Your comeback doesn't begin with force.
It begins with surrender.

CHAPTER 1

The Pivot I Never Saw Coming

Picture this.

Sterile white walls. Red alarms flashing against the glow of monitors. The crash cart pulled close, messy with opened vials and syringes. The air was so sharp with antiseptic it nearly stung.

Her body was failing. Doctors whispered about odds, less than ten percent. Her family stood by, bracing for goodbyes.

And then, a scream.

Not a polite, composed cry. A raw, guttural sound ripped from her son's chest. Twenty years old, watching his mother slip away.

Somewhere in that chaos, her eyes opened.

That woman in the hospital bed was me.

It is a little strange to me that this single defining moment of my life can be summed up in four words: "She opened her eyes."

So much is packed into those words. They tell a story of a fight, that I was not finished with life yet. They show how God stepped in, using the Holy Spirit through my son's scream to pull me back. They reveal a family who refused to give up, who knew deep down I was not done being a wife, a mother, or an Oma.

Those four words hold everything: grit, grace, toughness, and a miracle.

What none of us knew that day was just how long and winding the road ahead would be.

This was not where I had imagined life taking me. Just days before, I had been living in full color, heels clicking across polished floors, Pilates toning my muscles, a thriving business, and a sweet marriage humming in rhythm. Now, everything around me was washed in gray.

And yet, in that moment, something shifted. My will to survive locked in like instinct. But deeper still, my will to live ignited.

Because survival was not the end of my story, it was the beginning of a new chapter.

Your pivot may not look like mine. Maybe it came through loss, upheaval, or exhaustion. Or maybe it was the quiet kind of pivot, the moment you realized the life you built no longer fits.

This book is not about sickness or hospitals. It is about what happens when the life you knew gets ripped away and you are forced onto an unexpected path. It is about not mistaking survival for the finish line.

The year I turned fifty, life felt golden. Pilates three times a week, a business I had poured my heart into was flourishing, my kids were growing and finding their way, and a marriage that had weathered storms and settled into sweetness. After years of searching for balance, I had found my stride.

And then, in a blink, my body turned foreign.

It started with fatigue in my legs. The kind you dismiss with a laugh, I just need more sleep. But rest did not fix it. The weakness spread like ink in water.

The next clear memory is being loaded into an ambulance. Fluorescent lights streaked across my vision as paramedics fired questions I could not answer. My body was shutting down while my mind scrambled to catch up.

For three weeks, I remember nothing. Life carried on without me.

But in the ICU, I dreamed.

It was vivid, unsettling, and so real that even now I can close my eyes and see it.

I was trapped in a small, windowless room with no way out. A computer screen glowed in front of me. Suddenly, the flatline appeared. A second screen lit up, faint like a chance at hope, but then it too flatlined.

Panic rose in me. This is it. Tammy Gibson ceases to exist. No one will ever find me now.

I was not dead. I was erased. Lost.

And just when despair settled like a weight on my chest, I could feel motion around me, like hands rebuilding what had fallen apart. The air buzzed with quiet urgency. And then, through the haze, a face came into focus. Larry, my husband.

Relief hit like a flood. You found me.

Later, I learned those dreams may have coincided with the moments doctors shocked my heart back into rhythm. Twice.

That is the truth about survival. It does not feel heroic. It feels like surrender. Terrifying. Confusing. Wildly out of your control.

And yet, even there, God threads reminders through the chaos. A prayer whispered at your bedside. A loved one's face breaking through the blur. A quiet presence that says: your story is not finished.

In those moments, one verse echoed like a steady drumbeat in the background of my fear:
"Even though I walk through the darkest valley, I will fear no evil, for you are with me." Psalm 23:4

I finally understood why this was one of my grandpa's favorite Bible verses. It was not a promise that I would be spared from the valley. It was a reminder that I would not walk it alone.

Later, I also learned the full weight of what had happened.

I had experienced a rare reaction to COVID that caused multiple organ failure. By the time I was finally discharged, I had not just survived a hospital stay. I was living with kidney failure, nerve damage, and profound physical loss that I will never fully understand.

This was my pivot. Yours will look different. But the truth is the same: survival is not the end. It is the invitation to discover how to live again.

Reflection for You

When life pivots, it rarely asks your permission. Sometimes it shatters in an instant; other times it unravels slowly until one day you wake up in a story you do not recognize. But here is the hope: your pivot is not where the story ends. It is where a new chapter begins.

- What was the pivot you never saw coming?
- How did it shift the way you saw yourself or your future?
- Looking back, where can you see God's presence woven in, even if you did not recognize it at the time?

CHAPTER 2

Life or Limb

Thirty-three days into my hospital stay, I heard the words that turned my world on its axis.

"You are going to lose your leg."

Wait. What?

The words hit like static, loud and disorienting and impossible to process. I was so heavily medicated that I did not even realize something was wrong with my legs. I blinked at the doctor, certain I had misheard.

Then I looked at Larry. His face was pale but steady, carrying a truth he never wanted to say out loud.

"Tammy," he said gently, "if you want to live, they need to amputate your leg."

The air went out of the room.

My mind scrambled to catch up. Just a month earlier, I had been the woman in motion, heels clicking across floors, full of plans, strong legs carrying me everywhere I wanted to go. And now, in this sterile room, I was being told I would lose one of them.

The tissue in my leg had become infected after a series of medical procedures. The doctors had tried everything to stop it, but the infection had spread too far. Amputation was the final hope to save my life.

I had a choice: life or limb.

I wish I could tell you I processed that moment with wisdom and clarity. But there is no preparing for a sentence that will alter your body and your story forever. Death was not an option. Leaving my kids and leaving Larry was not even a question. I chose life.

But choosing life did not erase fear. It did not erase grief.

Lying there, staring at the ceiling tiles, I wondered, What will I look like? How will I walk? Will I still be me?

I had no reference point for this. No one teaches you how to say goodbye to a part of yourself.

The woman I had always been, the one who ran and climbed and led and carried and moved, was about to be reshaped in ways I could not yet imagine.

The morning of the surgery, the room felt too bright, too cold, too still. Nurses moved efficiently, their voices low and kind. Larry held my hand until the moment they wheeled me away. I studied his face, my constant through the chaos, and whispered, "I will see you soon."

Then the doors closed.

The anesthesia hit like a curtain falling between two acts of a play. When I woke up, I was in the second act. My right leg was gone.

I remember staring down at the space where it had been, blank at first, then flooded. The reality washed over me slowly, as if my brain needed permission to catch up. I did not cry. Not at first. It was too big for tears.

There was pain, yes, but mostly there was absence.

It is a strange thing to grieve something that is both physical and symbolic. My leg was not just flesh and bone. It was freedom, movement, autonomy, confidence. Losing it felt like losing my independence, my identity, my sense of being whole.

Grief did not hit all at once. It came in waves.

There were moments of disbelief, waking up thinking I could get out of bed, only to look down and remember. Moments of anger when phantom pain pulsed through the part of me that no longer existed. Moments of gratitude too, because I was alive when I should not have been.

My family tried to process it in their own ways. Larry never let me see him break, but I could read the exhaustion in his eyes. My kids hovered between love and fear, wanting to help but not knowing how. My parents prayed constantly. Everyone was doing their best to be strong, and I did not want to make it harder for them.

So I smiled when they walked in. I chatted with the nurses and anyone who came through my door. The stimulation and lightness were good for my soul and a welcome distraction from my circumstances.

I put on a brave face and said, "Just call me Bionic Tammy."

It was not denial. I was dealing with it the only way I knew how, with faith that everything would somehow be alright.

But when the room was quiet, the tears came. Not "why me" tears, but "what now" tears?

In that question, what now, was a turning point I did not yet understand.

I would come to see that moment as the beginning of rebuilding. The moment when the woman who lost so much began to find something deeper: strength that did not depend on perfection, beauty that did not rely on symmetry, and worth that did not hinge on what was missing.

The truth is, we all face our own amputations. Yours may not involve surgery or hospitals, but maybe you have had to cut away something to survive, a relationship, a job, a dream, an old version of yourself.

Amputation, by definition, is the removal of something damaged or diseased to preserve what is still alive. It is the separation of what once served you from what no longer can.

Letting go is not always clean or easy. Sometimes it feels like you are losing a part of yourself. But healing begins when you realize that release is not rejection. It is renewal.

When I chose to let my leg go, I was not giving up. I was blessing and releasing something that could no longer sustain me. It had carried me as far as it could, and then it was time to trust God with what came next.

And maybe that is true for you too. Some things are not meant to stay forever. Sometimes the bravest, most faith-filled act is to bless what once was and let it go.

Reflection for You

Life has a way of asking us to release what we thought we could not live without. Sometimes it is sudden, other times gradual, but it always demands courage. What you let go of may change how you see yourself, but it does not change who you truly are.

- What have you had to release in order to live?
- How has the loss of a person, role, or identity, reshaped your understanding of purpose?
- What does choosing life look like for you right now?

CHAPTER 3

When the Tides Turn

Within twenty-four hours of arriving at the ER, my kidneys had shut down. The doctors discovered severe rhabdomyolysis, meaning my muscle tissue was breaking down and flooding my system with toxins faster than my body could clear them. It explained the sudden weakness in my legs, but it was only a clue, not a full diagnosis. Dialysis became my lifeline.

At first, it was all a blur of machines and masked faces. Tubes snaking from my body. Numbers flashing across monitors. Words like stage four and failure spoken in tones careful enough that I knew I was not supposed to panic.

And then came a flicker of hope. In my third month in the hospital, my kidneys began to recover.

The doctor who had quietly shared his hopes for improvement fist-pumped Larry in the hallway. He called it remarkable. I called it a miracle.

Even so, when I was finally discharged, my kidneys were still in stage four. A transplant was "more when than if." My cousin Chad immediately offered to be a donor when I asked him. His *yes* alone felt like hope in human form.

As I stabilized, twice-weekly dialysis became routine. Outpatient meant 3 a.m. appointments, expensive transportation, and Larry attempting a few hours of sleep in his truck while I sat tethered to the machine. Every treatment drained me. I left hollowed, my strength siphoned along with the toxins.

But little by little, something else began to shift. I started noticing the way I spoke to myself in those in-between moments, the quiet after treatment, the stillness before sleep. My inner voice was harsh, impatient, always asking, Why are you not stronger by now?

So I began to change the conversation.

Instead of shaming myself for what I could not do, I started whispering, "Yes, this is hard. And you are still showing up."

That small act of self-compassion softened the edges of survival. It was not resignation; it was acceptance of what was true. And with acceptance came strength, not the loud, triumphant kind, but a quiet, enduring strength that let me keep moving forward.

But I was not willing to simply accept inevitability. Larry and I researched tirelessly. We found the best kidney specialist, overhauled my diet, increased my water intake, added creatine to aid muscle rebuilding since I was strictly limited on protein, and even listened to binaural beats for kidney healing. It was exhausting, but it worked.

Over the next eighteen months, my kidney function improved beyond every expectation. My doctor shook her head in disbelief and called it a miracle. She had never seen a recovery like mine. Aside from surviving in the first place, this was the greatest miracle of my journey.

That is the thing about healing, whether physical or emotional. Sometimes it is not all or nothing. Sometimes it is one small step layered on another until, one day, you realize you are standing on ground you were not sure you would ever see again.

Reflection for You

Maybe your challenge is not kidneys or hospitals. Maybe it is a career setback, a strained relationship, or a long season of feeling stuck. Whatever it looks like, the truth is the same. You cannot always control what happens, but you can choose how you respond. Healing often comes as a partnership, your effort joined with God's grace.

- Where in your life have you quietly accepted *"this is just the way it is"*?
- What's one small step you could take this week toward healing, growth, or change?
- How might faith and action together open space for God to rewrite your story?

CHAPTER 4

Coming Home to a Stranger

Quiet tears slid down my cheeks as the medical transport van pulled up in front of our house. One hundred and twenty-seven days. That's how long I had waited for this moment.

The sky outside seemed impossibly bright without the filter of hospital windows. It was a cloudy February day, but to me it looked radiant.

Larry and our two kids were with me. Waiting outside as we pulled up was my stepdaughter, Lesley, her husband, Rob, their three-year-old son, Grayson, and their brand-new puppy who eventually curled up and fell asleep at the foot of my wheelchair. It brought me so much joy to see them all gathered, three generations under one roof, laughter mixing with the relief of simply being together again.

Inside, the house looked both familiar and foreign. A new tile floor covered the downstairs, smooth and easy for the wheelchair to glide over. Ramps had been strategically placed inside and outside, transforming our once two-level world into one I could now navigate. The first-floor bathroom had been remodeled to be ADA compliant, funded by the generous donations from the GoFundMe fundraiser that had carried us through those hospital months.

My office, now my bedroom, had been thoughtfully converted for comfort and accessibility. A friend had decorated it with a plush comforter to soften the harsh lines of the rented hospital bed, and a "Welcome Home" sign hung above the door like a banner of victory and relief.

Even the Christmas tree still stood in the living room, two months past the holiday, its twinkling lights left up so I could enjoy them when I came home. Our dogs circled me at the door, tails wagging, though our chihuahua turned his head away, angry I'd been gone so long.

It was all so beautiful, thoughtful touches from people who loved me, reminders that life had gone on while I was away. And yet, home felt unfamiliar.

It should have been pure joy. Instead, it was joy braided with fear. Because the woman coming home wasn't the same woman who had left.

The Weight Carried by Caregivers

Before I share more of what those early days were like for me, I need to honor something that often gets overlooked in stories like mine. It is something I did not fully understand until I was the one lying in the bed while the people I loved stood beside it.

Caregiving, especially for someone whose life is tied to your own, is the hardest job in the world.

There are wounds the patient never sees.
There are memories the survivor never carries.
There are moments the caregivers will never forget.

While I was fighting to stay alive, the people who loved me were fighting a different kind of battle. One without medication for the pain. One without nurses to guide them. One without rest or reassurance. They were asked to be steady in moments that would have undone them if they had allowed themselves to feel everything at once.

Larry carried the weight of those months in the hospital.
He witnessed things I did not see.
He heard conversations I was not awake for.
He made decisions when his heart was breaking.

He kept showing up when he had nothing left.
He absorbed trauma so I could survive mine.

That leaves a mark. A quiet, permanent one.

And once I came home, though the daily tasks shifted to my mom, Larry did not step back.

He stepped in again.

Every evening after work, he came home and picked up wherever my mom left off—lifting, transferring, cleaning, organizing medications, tending to my wounds, adjusting medical equipment, helping me into bed, soothing fears in the night, protecting my spirit when I was too tired to protect it myself.

On weekends, it was all hands on deck.
He took over the feedings.
He helped with dressing changes.
He pushed my chair, helped me stand, learned every machine, every alarm, every new need.
He carried the emotional weight of being my partner while learning the physical labor of being my caregiver.

It was not a one-person effort.

It was a family effort.
A team effort.
A whole-household effort.

Once I came home, my mom became the day-in, day-out caregiver.
She stepped into a role no parent imagines for their adult child.
She prepared tube feedings, crushed medications, cleaned and flushed lines, managed alarms, changed wound dressings, and stayed alert even

when she was exhausted. She lived in a state of constant vigilance because she could not afford not to.

She held my days together.
Larry held my evenings, my nights, and my weekends.
Together, they held me.

And my dad held my mom.

Every night, after the house finally quieted, she would call him. He became her emotional caregiver from afar. He steadied her when she cried. He reassured her when fear rose. He processed the day with her. He carried her so she could keep carrying me.

Children step into caregiving roles long before they feel ready.
My kids learned to hold responsibility and fear at the same time.
They helped in small ways that were actually enormous.
They loved me through every fragile moment.

Caregiving reshapes a person from the inside out. It creates invisible scars. It demands strength that feels profound and unsettling. It asks a person to love beyond their capacity and give beyond what is reasonable.

If you have been the caregiver, I want you to hear this: I see you.
You carried what someone else could not.
You stood when everything inside you was trembling.
You learned new forms of bravery without ever asking for them.
You held together what felt like it was falling apart.
You loved with a force that kept someone alive.

And if you have been cared for by someone you love, like I was, let your heart make room for what they endured. Not with guilt. Not with apology. With honor.

Because there are two kinds of strength in every survival story:

The strength of the one who fought to live.

And the strength of the ones who fought to keep them here.

Both deserve to be named.

Both deserve tenderness.

Both made this chapter of my life possible.

When Home Doesn't Feel Like Home Yet

At first, I wasn't really living. I was observing. Watching life happen to me, feedings, wound care, showers, medications, without being an active participant.

A Hoyer lift scooped me out of bed and swung me through the air like cargo before lowering me into a shower chair. Sometimes I called it my "wild ride," trying to inject humor into the process. But once the chair rolled under the spray, the humor faded.

The first shower Larry helped me with on his own took nearly four hours from start to finish. Four hours of carefully wrapping my wounds and tubes in waterproof film, only to later peel back layer after layer of damp medical tape, slowly and painfully, trying not to disturb the fragile skin underneath. Even the gentle pressure of the water irritated my skin, turning what once felt like comfort into another test of endurance.

Larry moved carefully and tenderly, masking his exhaustion behind steady focus. By the time he wheeled me back to bed, we were both drained. He was worn out from the sheer physical labor, and I was exhausted from the emotional weight of needing so much help.

After that, we decided to bring in home health aides for shower days. It was too much for one person to manage, no matter how much love fueled the effort.

There I was, naked and vulnerable, being scrubbed by complete strangers. Some were gentle and aware of the intimacy of the moment. Others were not, their brisk hands and rushed voices reminding me how powerless I was. But even in those awkward, humbling moments, I found a strange kind of grace. Their hands, whether kind or hurried, were still helping me heal. Every act of care, no matter how uncomfortable, was an act of love in motion.

When the lift carried me back to bed, exhaustion hit so hard I often slept the rest of the day. A simple shower felt like a marathon for me and for whoever was assisting that day.

My left leg was covered in open wounds that needed daily dressing changes. The process was slow, meticulous, and painful. Each time the bandages were peeled away, I saw more evidence of a body I no longer recognized.

A feeding tube tethered me constantly. Bottles of pills were ground up and funneled through it during the day, while liquid nutrients flowed into me through the night. If the tubing kinked, the machine alarm shrieked in the dark, jolting us awake until someone untangled it.

Even the connection with my husband looked different. When Larry called home on his lunch breaks, I couldn't hold the phone to my ear. I would put him on speaker, his voice filling the room while I whispered back, too weak to lift my arms.

This was my life. Stripped down. Stripped of independence. Stripped of dignity.

I had once been the woman who ran businesses, managed schedules, and carried the weight of a household on her shoulders. Now I couldn't brush my own teeth. And underneath the daily grind, one question pulsed in me like a heartbeat: Who am I now?

My family and I were walking through the same story, yet each of us experienced it in our own way. We processed differently, coped differently, and showed up differently. Some leaned into doing. Some into faith. Some into distraction. Some into quiet strength. There was no right or wrong, only love expressed in unique forms. We respected each other's process and held space for one another even when our emotions took different shapes.

As for me, I was numb at first, exhausted, simply adjusting. But as I regained strength, I made a choice. I tried to keep a peaceful, hopeful spirit for my family, knowing they were finally beginning to exhale after months of living on adrenaline. They mirrored that hope back to me. I shed plenty of tears too, but I didn't waste time on "why me." My question was always: "what now"?

Slowly, I began to see that maybe God wasn't asking me to claw my way back to the woman I had been, the one who, just four months earlier at fifty, finally felt like she had found her stride. Maybe He was asking me to trust that His story for me wasn't finished, and that He could still make beauty from what felt broken.

That is the paradox of any pivot. You expect relief when the storm passes, but what often greets you is a stranger staring back in the mirror. And yet, even there, God's voice cuts through the confusion: You are still mine. You are still loved. You are still here.

Reflection for You

Losing independence does not always look like hospital beds and feeding tubes. Sometimes it looks like heartbreak that steals your confidence, burnout that drains your energy, or the slow erosion of joy until you barely recognize yourself. Whatever form it takes, the feeling is the same: stripped, reduced, uncertain of who you are now.

But here is the hope. You are not your circumstances. The version of you staring back in the mirror is not the end of the story. It is the beginning of renewal.

- Have you ever found yourself in a season where you didn't recognize the woman in the mirror?
- What parts of your identity have you been clinging to that no longer fit?
- How might God be inviting you to release the old and step into who you are becoming now?

CHAPTER 5

Learning to Stand Again

A few weeks later, I found my first answer to the lingering *what now* when I stood again.

The first time I stood after returning home, it felt like the earth tilted beneath me.

My therapist crouched close, looping a gait belt around my waist. I wrapped both hands around his forearms as he braced and lifted. My left leg, the one that had endured so much, trembled under me, but he held steady.

And then, I was up.

My body swayed, my balance uncertain, but I was standing. My mom and son clapped and cheered from the corner of the room. My face broke into a wide smile. There were no tears this time. It was pride. Joy. Life.

It had been months since I had seen the world from that height. Months since I had felt what it was like to bear my own weight, even if only for a few seconds.

That day, something inside me shifted. My body was still weak, but my spirit was standing tall.

In that moment, I felt God's presence steadying me as much as my therapist's arms. It was as if Heaven whispered, "See, you are still capable of rising". That awareness filled me with a quiet confidence, proof that His strength really is made perfect in our weakness.

Rehab became my full-time job.

After three months in the hospital and one in acute inpatient rehab, I transitioned home for five months of therapy before moving into outpatient care. Every phase was a new mountain.

Before each session, I felt the same mix of excitement and dread. I never knew how much it would hurt, how much I could accomplish, or how much progress I would make. It was like going to the dentist, you brush and floss, but somehow, there is still a cavity. I felt guilty for not doing more, for not healing faster, for not being stronger.

I put so much pressure on myself to perform. My mind was determined, but my body was not always ready to cooperate. These moments were often conversations with God, seeking His peace and strength when mine fell short.

Still, I loved therapy days. My sessions became social sessions. My team was kind, encouraging, and endlessly patient.

The stimulation and conversation reminded me that I was more than a patient. I was still me.

Three months after I stood, I was fit for my first prosthetic.

I had built up that moment in my head like it was the grand finale, the day everything would click back into place. I imagined sliding it on, standing up tall, and walking out of the clinic like a heroine in a comeback montage.

Reality was less cinematic.

The socket pinched. The weight felt wrong. My muscles, still rebuilding, were not strong enough to keep up. Even with help, I could barely balance. The pain was sharp and relentless. I left exhausted, my body sore and my heart disappointed.

But I kept trying.

My Orthotics and Prosthetics team became a highlight of those long clinic days. I loved these guys, part artist and part engineer. Their ability to problem-solve was matched only by their patience with my endless questions and requests. I did not always know what I needed or wanted. I was new to prosthetic life, after all.

For six months, I worked to make that prosthetic fit my life. It was functional but not comfortable. It allowed me to walk, but only in small doses. The frustration of wanting freedom but being limited by pain was real.

Then, we tried something new: an adjustable socket model.

The technology was incredible. For the first time, I could adjust the fit myself, which made putting it on so much easier. It was bulkier and heavier than my first model, far from ideal, but I was willing to endure the extra weight for the flexibility it offered.

I did not expect to use that socket for long. I ended up wearing it for nearly two years.

Eventually, I transitioned into a lighter, sleeker version that felt more natural and less like a piece of equipment. Each upgrade was like another step toward reclaiming parts of my identity, one layer of limitation peeled away at a time.

But there was another challenge waiting, my left foot.

Because I had lost the soleus muscle in my calf due to infected tissue, my ankle had limited mobility. To walk safely, I needed an AFO brace to stabilize it. But first, my leg had to heal. The surgical wounds were deep, and recovery took time.

While waiting, I wore a therapeutic walking boot for support. It was not pretty, but it worked. Each small adaptation, every brace and socket and adjustment, was a reminder that rebuilding is not about going back to what was. It is about learning how to move forward differently.

Rehab taught me patience in motion.

It is one thing to lose something, it is another to rebuild your life around that loss. There were days I dreaded the process, days I wanted to call in sick, and days I found myself laughing through the pain with the people who helped me rise again.

It was not glamorous. But it was transformative.

Because healing is not about speed, it is about staying in the process long enough to let strength find you.

I learned that God does not rush the process, He refines it. Every slow, shaky repetition was an act of trust, a chance to lean on His strength instead of my own.

Reflection for You

Sometimes healing feels like starting over with training wheels. You want to sprint, but life hands you a walker. You crave the final outcome, but growth hides in the daily work. The truth is, the comeback never happens all at once, it is a thousand little victories strung together with faith and grit.

- What "rehab season" are you in right now, physically, emotionally, or spiritually?
- Where are you pressuring yourself to go faster than your healing allows?
- How could you celebrate progress today, even if it feels small?

CHAPTER 6

The Identity Comeback

For four months, in the hospital and rehab, I avoided mirrors.

I could feel enough to know I wasn't ready to see knotted hair, flaking skin, scabs, tubes, wounds. My body had endured more than I ever imagined it could.

It was easier to look forward than to look at what had been stripped away.

A few weeks after coming home, I finally faced the mirror.

The woman staring back startled me. Cheeks hollowed by months of malnutrition, hair a jagged mix of new growth and cropped-out knots. I looked fragile, yes, but more than that, unfamiliar.

That first look brought a single question to my lips:
"Who am I now, God?"

I asked it often in those early days. I did not recognize the body that bore the scars of survival, yet somewhere deep inside I knew I was still His. A child of God. That was the only identity that had not changed.

And then I remembered the dream.

While sedated in the ICU, I had seen myself standing on a stage before a crowd, strong, radiant, alive. Larry stood beside me, tears in his eyes. It felt like a mountaintop moment, a vision too vivid to forget.

That dream became my compass. Even before I could stand again, God had already shown me what I was rising toward.

As strength slowly returned, my world began to expand beyond survival mode.

Being Seen Again

After months of being hidden away in hospital and rehab rooms, it was time to enter back into the world and be seen.

Any time I went out, prosthetic or not, I felt the eyes.

Some people smiled warmly. "You're doing great!"
Others tried not to look at all.

Children stared, curious and unfiltered, asking, "What happened to her?" while parents flushed with embarrassment and whispered, "She was in an accident," the easiest explanation.

I never minded curiosity. I preferred it to silence. I wanted people to ask, to see, to understand that resilience doesn't look the same on everyone. We all carry scars, some seen and some unseen, and each one tells a story of strength.

Mine tell quite a few.

I have more than eleven distinct scars from my original hospital stay and another ten or more from foot surgery. Some are large, like the nine-inch scars that run down either side of my left calf. Others are small, like the thin line from my chest tube. Each one is a reminder of what my body endured and of the grace that carried me through.

In those early months, most of my outings were to doctor appointments or therapy sessions. The neuro physical therapy clinic became my second home. Surrounded by others facing challenges even greater than mine, I didn't feel out of place. I felt grateful.

Being seen again was uncomfortable at first, but it reminded me of something essential.

I was not a tragedy to be pitied.

I was a story still being written.

The Cost of Survival

Before anything could begin to heal, I had to grieve what I'd lost.

After months in the hospital, my hair had become one giant tangle of knots despite the efforts of sweet nurses who tried to comb it out. I was devastated. On top of losing my leg, I was losing my hair and with it, a part of my identity. Bald spots had formed, and one, shaped like a heart on the back of my head, never grew back.

One afternoon, a beautiful woman named Marsha came into my hospital room. With gentleness and care, she worked through the knots, cutting away what couldn't be saved. I cried quietly as she prayed with me, reminding me, "You're still you."

Her compassion touched me in a moment when I felt the most unlike myself.

It would take time for those words to sink in, but they became a quiet thread I carried into my recovery.

Graduations and Gratitude

By spring, as I was learning to live in my body again, life stretched beyond hospital walls.

The calendar filled with three family graduations, and I made it my mission to be at each one. I ordered a new dress for every ceremony, small symbols of fresh starts.

Fashion has always been part of my DNA. Color. Texture. Detail. During recovery, it became therapy. I learned that what I put on my body could shift what I believed about myself.

Each dress had requirements. Long enough to cover my amputation, which I was still self-conscious about. Loose enough to hide the tubes still coming out of my body. Easy to pull on and off, because I still needed help getting dressed.

My best friends arrived with bags of hats, knowing my hair had thinned from months of illness. I had never been a hat girl, but we laughed, tried them all on, and took pictures so I could see myself in them. They became a kind of armor, helping me face the world while covering what still needed time to heal.

The hats were temporary, like the feeding tube in my stomach or the dialysis port in my chest. Healing isn't always glamorous. Sometimes it's about embracing what helps you keep going.

Nick's college graduation came first. His entire class of thirteen students received their degrees in a small church ceremony. I watched my son cross the stage, his face full of pride and possibility. Any mother would have been emotional, but for me, the gratitude was overwhelming. Months earlier, I wasn't sure I would live to see that day.

Two more graduations followed. Montana's high school and Lesley's college.

I had missed so much of Montana's senior year, her entire basketball season, senior pictures, projects, and more. To be at her graduation was incredibly special. We shared laughs and tears, and I beamed as I listened to her deliver the heartfelt but funny speech she had written for her class.

Lesley balanced full-time work as a pediatric emergency department nurse, raising her son, finishing her BSN online, and supporting Larry and me throughout my hospital stay. Her accomplishment reflected determination and grace. Her husband, Rob, was her steady support, grounding their busy life with joy.

Each celebration carried joy and exhaustion. Each one was a miracle.

I watched my children step into their futures while I was still learning how to live again, and in that paradox, I found peace.

There are moments when love feels amplified, multiplied by everything you've endured to reach it. Those ceremonies were exactly that. Gratitude, awe, hope, and pride tangled together until they became something luminous.

Still Me

The dresses and hats I wore to graduations weren't about appearances. They were small acts of confidence. Each outfit said, I'm still me.

That truth ran deeper than I realized.

For thirteen years, I built a career as a fashion and beauty blogger. Style wasn't just something I enjoyed. It was a language I spoke fluently, ingrained in the fiber of who I am.

So when my body changed, that part of me grieved too. I had to relearn how to express myself through a body that didn't always cooperate. It broke my heart at times. But it also taught me grace, how to honor the woman I am now, not by erasing the past, but by adapting it.

Shoes have always been my favorite outfit detail.

So when foot surgery in April 2025 finally allowed me to wear a regular shoe without my AFO, it felt monumental. I had dreamed of the day I could choose a shoe for expression instead of necessity.

When I was ready, I went searching for something that matched who I am now. Strong. Resilient. Still a little glam.

After an extensive online search, I found them. Combat boots with sequins and studs.

Comfort first. Sparkle second.
A blend of grit and glam that finally felt like me.

Healing isn't about returning to who you were before.
It's about seeing yourself clearly, loving what you see, and realizing you were never lost.

Showing up with lip gloss or a favorite hat wasn't about appearances. It was about remembering that even in loss, I still had agency.

Seeing myself through God's eyes, whole, capable, still vibrant, helped me begin to rediscover myself.

An Extension of Me

As my strength returned, so did my sense of expression. Even my accessory options were opening up. About eighteen months after coming home, I received a grant from PossAbilities for a new wheelchair. I was thrilled, not just for the comfort and freedom it offered, but because it finally felt like an extension of me.

Until then, I had been using an insurance-issued chair. Black. Heavy. Practical. It did its job, but every time I looked at it, I felt like people saw the chair and not me. The slick metal rims slipped under my weakened hands, and the weight made ramps nearly impossible to navigate on my own. Every outing reminded me of what I'd lost.

It wasn't just uncomfortable. It was unlike me.

I didn't want to be seen in it, not because of vanity, but because it didn't reflect who I was. It made me feel small, dependent, muted.

The new chair was different.

It didn't just roll. It spoke.

The lighter frame moved easily beneath me. Rubber grip rims gave me control again. The frame was embossed with leopard print, and the wheels gleamed metallic red.

It said, *She's still here.*

The first time I caught my reflection in a window, I smiled. For the first time in a long while, I didn't see the chair first. I saw me.

The Refining Season

Recovery taught me endurance.
Rediscovery was teaching me grace.

I was no longer trying to get back to the woman I had been. She was gone, and that was okay. I was emerging stronger, freer, more grounded in faith.

That ICU dream still guides me. I sometimes joke that God gave me a trailer preview of my future. I can still see it clearly, me on stage, Larry by my side, strong and radiant.

God didn't just heal me. He redefined me.

I am still growing, still evolving, learning that identity is not static. It is a living testimony of what grace can do.

The woman I was before the storm had confidence.
The woman I am now has conviction.

And with that conviction came a quiet knowing.

My story was not meant to stay private.

It was meant to be shared.

Reflection for You

There comes a moment when survival gives way to rediscovery, when the question shifts from *Will I make it?* to *Who am I now?*

- Where in your story are you learning to see yourself with new eyes?
- What parts of your identity have shifted, and how might God be shaping something beautiful through that change?
- Can you bless who you were, honor who you are, and trust who you are becoming?

You don't have to look exactly like you once did to recognize yourself again.

Sometimes the comeback is the woman staring back in the mirror, wiser, weathered, and radiant with grace.

CHAPTER 7

Called to Rise

At first, I only shared updates so people would know I was still alive.

While I was in the hospital, my family created a private Facebook group to keep others informed about my condition.

During those early hospital days, a friend's nine-year-old daughter made beaded bracelets that said Tough Like Tammy. She passed them out at a prayer vigil to remind people to pray for me.

That sweet act of love became a rally cry, and soon I had a community from around the world lifting me up daily. We called them Team Tough Like Tammy, or Team TLT. That simple bracelet became a symbol of hope and unity long before it became a brand.

When I was finally home and strong enough to use my iPad with a single finger, I began sharing small pieces of my journey on Instagram, snippets of recovery, flashes of gratitude, little victories that marked the distance between who I had been and who I was becoming.

Each post was honest but practical. I was not trying to inspire anyone; I was simply sharing what was happening. What I did not realize was that honesty has a way of creating ripples.

Messages began to appear. Some were brief notes of encouragement, others long paragraphs from people who saw themselves in my story. Many said things like, "You remind me to keep going," or "Your courage gives me hope." Those words touched me, but the real connection came in the quiet corners of my DMs.

That is where I met Kyra and Greg, two other amputees navigating recovery in real time. Kyra was in Germany, Greg in Texas. Different continents, different hospitals, but similar scars and fears. Our conversations were raw and unfiltered in a way only people who have been through it can understand.

We traded photos, milestones, frustrations, and small triumphs. Over time, the updates became check-ins. How is the leg today? Still walking every day? How are you adjusting?

We may never meet in person, but they are part of my story now, a reminder that connection is not limited by distance. Sometimes healing happens through messages that cross oceans.

As my strength returned, I began sharing more openly. Lives, reels, Q&As, digital windows into life after limb loss. I was comfortable on camera; years of business and brand work had taught me how to communicate. What I had to learn was how much to communicate.

In the beginning, I overshared, offering medical terms, surgical details, wound-care explanations. I thought clarity was kindness, but I quickly noticed the glazed eyes and polite nods. People wanted the human story, not the medical chart. I learned to pull back, to focus on what they could relate to, perseverance, humor, faith, and daily life.

That balance, truth without oversharing, became a new skill. It taught me that storytelling is stewardship.

Then came the invitation to host an Instagram series highlighting other amputees.

Every conversation left me changed. A father who lost his leg in a motorcycle accident but still coached his child's soccer team. A young woman who played for her country's adapted soccer team and launched her modeling career. Another who climbed rock walls with a prosthetic and taught others to do the same.

Their resilience mirrored my own, yet their experiences reminded me that no two recoveries are the same.

What united us was the desire to educate and encourage, to replace pity with understanding.

The more we talked, the more I realized this was not about disability at all. It was about possibility.

Those interviews became a kind of ministry, though I did not label it that way. Purpose does not always need a title. Sometimes it simply looks like showing up, listening, and letting your scars speak for themselves.

A few months later, a local high school invited me to share my story.

The event was held in the library, rows of folding chairs between the shelves, sunlight filtering through tall windows. The students were quiet at first, polite but guarded. Then, as I spoke, their faces softened. They leaned in.

Their questions were thoughtful and genuine. How does the prosthetic work? Does it hurt? How long did it take to walk again? They were not afraid to ask what most adults tiptoed around. Their curiosity disarmed me.

Time passed faster than I expected. When the bell rang, I felt a mix of gratitude and joy. I remember thinking, I could do this over and over again.

That moment confirmed what I had already begun to sense online. I was not just sharing a story. I was teaching, connecting, helping people see life differently.

Since then, I have spoken not only to high school students but also to classes of physical-therapy assistants and orthotics-and-prosthetics students. Their questions are technical about angles, sockets, and balance, but what they really want to understand is experience.

Book learning builds knowledge. Hearing a patient's voice builds empathy. I love bridging that gap, helping future professionals see that behind every diagnosis is a person learning to live again.

Each time I speak, I feel a familiar rhythm: gratitude, excitement, purpose. It is never about applause; it is about exchange. I give my story, and somehow I receive healing in return.

I did not set out to become a speaker by accident. I knew deep down it was what God was calling me to do. That vision He gave me, the one I saw so vividly in the ICU, was not just a dream. It was direction. My only job now was to stay obedient and keep saying yes, one opportunity at a time.

The more I spoke, the more something inside me settled.

Every conversation, every connection, every word spoken aloud became part of my recovery.

I began to understand that calling does not always show up with fanfare or certainty. Sometimes it begins as a whisper, a quiet nudge that keeps returning until you finally decide to answer it.

That is what speaking became for me: my answer.

Reflection for You

Purpose does not always begin with a grand revelation. Sometimes it starts with a single step, a post, a conversation, a "yes" whispered through fear.

- What truth might you share that could give someone else courage?
- Where could you turn your own lessons into light for others?
- What if your story, the one you have been hesitant to tell, is the very thing God intends to use?

You don't have to have it all figured out to begin.
You just have to begin.

CHAPTER 8

Obedience in Action

The room glowed softly beneath the chandeliers, the hum of conversation rising above the clinking of glasses. It was a warm summer evening at the country club, one of those nights when everything feels possible. Guests dressed in white filled the tables, laughter mingling with the music, anticipation building for what was about to unfold.

After months of planning, the PossAbilities Fashion Show and Dinner was finally here.

The event was a fundraiser for PossAbilities, a nonprofit that supports individuals with physical disabilities and veterans through adaptive activities, community events, and grants. I had been part of the planning committee since April, and every detail mattered, especially when it came to the models. Each one was a member of the program, each living with a different disability. Some used prosthetics, others walked with canes or AFOs, and several used wheelchairs.

My role was to secure clothing donations from local boutiques and adaptive brands. I wanted each model to feel confident and celebrated, not "accommodated." We worked hard to find pieces that fit well, moved easily, and reflected the model's personality. Watching them try on clothes was one of my favorite parts of the entire process. Smiles, laughter, and a sense of belonging filled the room.

When the final selections were made, we could feel something special taking shape. This was not just a fashion show; it was a statement. Style belongs to everyone.

On the night of the show, I wore a white wrap dress for the first half of the evening and later changed into the black gown that had been featured on the event invitation. Being photographed for that invitation was surreal, a small but powerful reminder that the woman who had once spent months in a hospital bed was now part of something vibrant, creative, and alive.

When the event began, I was introduced and then took the microphone to share my story. In the room were several individuals who were in management roles at the clinics I had spent so much time at over the previous few years. It was gratifying for them to hear another story of a patient their clinics were helping.

Afterward, the models made their first runway appearance, followed by dinner service, and then a second round of looks. The energy in the room was joyful, supportive, and full of celebration. Each model owned their moment, beaming as the crowd cheered them on.

I was so proud of that evening, not just because it was a success, but because it brought visibility and confidence to people who do not often get the spotlight. It also raised important funds to continue the mission of PossAbilities.

It was not the first time I had been before an audience since my amputation, but it was the first time I had returned to the world of fashion. The first time I had ever MC'd an event.

When it was all over, I felt exhilarated, proud, and completely exhausted in the best possible way.

That night was more than a fundraiser. It was a full-circle moment, blending who I had been with who I am now. I had spent years teaching women how to show up with confidence, but this time it meant something deeper. We were not modeling clothes; we were modeling resilience.

A couple months later, I was honored to be recognized as **PossAbilities' Member of the Year** for my involvement in organizing the fashion show and helping bring the vision to life. The honor was not just a glass award to display on my shelf, as beautiful as it was. It was a reflection of every volunteer hour, every conversation, every moment spent believing that visibility matters. Standing on that stage, surrounded by people who had cheered me through so many milestones, I felt an overwhelming sense of gratitude. What began as an evening of recognition had turned into something far greater, a celebration of community, confidence, and the power of showing up.

It was more than recognition; it was confirmation. The doors I had once prayed for were beginning to open, one opportunity at a time.

My First Keynote

Nine months later, I found myself rolling through the glass doors of the Anaheim Convention Center, the buzz of voices and the scent of essential oils filling the air. The expo was in full swing, booths lined with wellness resources, journals, and self-care essentials. It was the kind of environment where calm and curiosity coexisted.

I was there to deliver my first in-person keynote titled "The Joyful Path to Resilience."

The organizers had a small stage at the front of the room. It did not have a ramp, so I parked my wheelchair just below it, handheld mic in my lap, scanning the forty-five or so people who had gathered. They were a mix of men and women, attendees still in yoga clothes, mats tucked under their arms, faces expectant and relaxed.

My husband, son, and brother-in-law joined me, their smiles both comforting and grounding. I took a deep breath and reminded myself: This is obedience, not performance.

When the time came, I began. The words flowed easily at first, stories of recovery, faith, and the five emotions that helped me rebuild my life. The audience nodded, smiled, even laughed in the right moments. Their warmth steadied me. Twice, I lost my place completely, my mind going blank, but I regrouped quickly and kept going. Let me tell you, keynotes are not for the faint of heart. For a forty-minute keynote with no notes, I counted that a victory.

As I spoke, I felt that familiar peace rise within me, the one that whispers, You are exactly where you are supposed to be.

When I finished, the applause was gentle but heartfelt. A few attendees came up afterward to thank me for sharing my story. One woman said, "I came for yoga but I think I found perspective instead." Another woman asked when I was going to write a book, and I replied with a smile, "It's in the works."

Michelle, the event organizer, hugged me before I left. "You were wonderful," she said. "We would love to have you back next year."

I smiled, feeling both drained and deeply fulfilled. Public speaking had always been part of the vision God gave me in that ICU dream, and this felt like the first major step into it.

Driving home with my family that night, I watched the California sunset fade through the car window and thought, *This is what obedience feels like. Not easy, not flawless, but exactly right.*

That night also marked the beginning of a new season, one where sharing my story from a stage was not just healing for me; it became a calling. Over time, that calling evolved into what I do now as a keynote speaker, helping others find strength in their own stories and the courage to share them.

The Turning Point

That keynote became the defining moment of everything that came next.

The fashion show had rekindled my confidence; that first keynote confirmed my calling. It was not about chasing the next event or the biggest stage. It was about walking faithfully through every open door God placed in front of me.

From that day forward, Tough Like Tammy began to evolve from a personal story of survival into a mission: to empower others to rise from their challenges with strength, grace, and purpose. What started as a small community online at @ToughLikeTammy grew into a platform for connection, encouragement, and resilience.

I no longer saw my story as something to overcome. It was something to offer.

Each opportunity since has been an act of obedience, a chance to serve, to shine light, and to remind others that their hardest chapters can become the foundation of their greatest impact.

I do not know where every step will lead, but I do know this: I was never meant to just survive what happened to me. I was meant to use it.

Reflection for You

Your story may not include microphones, stages, or spotlights, but you still have an audience.

Someone needs to hear your truth to find the courage to face their own.

- Where is God asking you to step out of comfort and into calling?
- What opportunities might already be waiting for your "yes"?
- What part of your story is ready to be used for good?

Obedience isn't about perfection.

It's about partnership, with purpose, with growth, and with the One who can use anything, even our pain, for impact.

CHAPTER 9

Building the Mission

Momentum has a way of sneaking up on you. One day, you're wondering if you're doing enough. The next, you're living inside the answer.

After the expo, doors began opening that I had not gone searching for. Partnerships, invitations, interviews, it felt as if everything was expanding at once. But it did not happen overnight. Each opportunity arrived like a small whisper from God saying, Keep going. You are on the right path.

Purpose in Motion

By early 2025, Tough Like Tammy was no longer just a story of survival. It was becoming a movement of resilience and visibility.

The days were full and often a little messy. I spent my mornings at my desk with our two old dogs curled nearby, working on social media content, client projects, or new writing for my blog and book. Some afternoons were spent at physical therapy or the gym, continuing my own strength work.

After I started driving again, I would drive myself to appointments, loading my wheelchair into the car, still proud every time I managed it. Larry handled the bigger events, meetings, and speaking engagements, but the day-to-day logistics were mine. He would call during his lunch break, checking in like clockwork. Some days I sounded energized and inspired; others, just tired. But every day, there was movement.

And with that movement came momentum.

The first partnership of the year was with Citrus Valley Physical Therapy and Wellness, the gym that had cheered me through recovery and celebrated every milestone. They welcomed me into their community and supported my strength-building journey. They made me feel like their gym was my gym, celebrating my coming-home anniversary as one of their own. It meant more than I can fully express. They weren't just cheering from the sidelines. They were walking alongside me. They saw something in me that they wanted to encourage.

Soon after came SpinLife Mobility and the chance to represent their Baja Bandit scooter. It was not just a product; it was freedom on wheels. I loved showing people that mobility devices were not a symbol of limitation but a pathway to possibility.

Around that same time, I partnered with multiple adaptive fashion lines to showcase their thoughtful designs, functional pieces made for women with limited dexterity or adaptive needs. It was meaningful work that showed how confidence and accessibility can coexist beautifully.

I understood this firsthand. Getting dressed had become a whole new experience for me. I learned to avoid buttons, hooks, and anything hard to pull on. Adaptive fashion was not just practical; it restored a sense of independence and style I desperately missed.

Each collaboration carried meaning beyond promotion. These were not random brand deals. They were extensions of my message: that strength, confidence, and dignity belong to everyone. And every partnership introduced me to new women, new hearts, who resonated with the mission.

That summer, I was featured on multiple podcasts and media outlets, and by July, my face was on the cover of The Beauty Box Magazine.

The headline read: "Radiance in Independence: Bold Beauty, Fearless Freedom."

Inside, I shared how my journey through adversity sparked something deeper, a movement rooted in grace, grit, and purpose.

A few months later, I visited Loma Linda Hospital, the very place that had saved my life, and saw the new display I was nominated for, the "I Am Hallway." I knew it was coming, but seeing it in person was still surreal.

Beside my photo were the words: *I Am Tough.*

The wall featured stories of people who had survived the unimaginable, now offering hope to the patients and families walking through their own battles.

As I stood there, I vaguely recognized a familiar face walking toward me. After he passed, I turned to Larry and asked, "Was that my hospital chaplain?" He did not know, since he had never met him, but he tracked him down so I could be sure.

It was him. Seth, the chaplain who had visited and prayed with me during some of my hardest nights. We spoke for several minutes, and I had the opportunity to thank him for his kindness and his prayers.

Seeing him again, in that very hallway, felt like a quiet reminder of how God weaves people into our stories right when we need them most.

I stood there quietly, humbled, not just by the honor of being included, but by the full-circle grace of it all. God keeps surprising me. And I am just getting started.

The Confirmation

By October, I rolled onto the stage before more than 300 women at an annual Women's Conference, delivering my talk titled "Survival to Surrender: Meeting Jesus in My Hardest Season."

I wore a leopard-print pencil skirt, a black tee, and my sequined combat boots, the perfect mix of grit and glam.

As I spoke, I watched the audience lean in. I could see when something landed: the shift in posture, the silent tears, the quiet nods.

Afterward, women approached me, each one sharing what resonated most deeply. Many talked about struggling to show themselves compassion, about comparing their current selves to the person they used to be.

I could tell my story shocked them at first, the reality of all I had been through, but then I saw it transform into something else entirely. They were not looking at me with pity. They saw the evidence of God shining through me, and in that light, they recognized something of their own strength.

They saw possibility.

And that was what I wanted most. Not for them to see me, but to see what is possible when you let God rewrite what fear tried to erase.

The Quiet Work

Even as things grew outwardly, inwardly I wrestled with pressure, mostly the kind I put on myself.

Pain was my constant companion. Neuropathy in my left foot often felt like it was on fire. Contractures in my hip flexors from years of limited mobility made it difficult to stand fully upright, putting strain on my lower back. And then there was the phantom pain, an intense pulse of electricity that could strike without warning and linger on and off for hours.

Living with chronic pain taught me endurance in ways nothing else could. I had to pace myself, listen to my body, and accept that healing did not mean the absence of pain. It meant learning how to live well in the midst of it.

The medical costs, copays, prosthetic updates, mobility equipment, all of it added up. I wanted to help relieve the financial strain on my husband.

In God's timing, I was offered a part-time role as a marketing and outreach coordinator for an online coach. It was remote, flexible, and allowed me to use my creative skills again. That steady income felt like oxygen, relieving the immediate stress and giving me the freedom to focus on Tough Like Tammy without desperation.

Still, I spent countless hours rewriting my website, tweaking my Instagram bio, and redefining what the brand was really about. I kept feeling caught between two worlds: the one I came from, branding and visibility for entrepreneurs, and the one I was stepping into, resilience, growth, and faith.

There were days I felt like I was finding my voice all over again.

For months in the hospital, I had literally been muted, first by a ventilator and then by a tracheotomy. I remember trying to speak and only air coming out. The frustration and helplessness of wanting to communicate but having nothing audible left was overwhelming.

Later, in business, that silence returned in a different form, a muted confidence I did not recognize at first. I would scroll through social media and second-guess what to say on my own account,

@ToughLikeTammy, wondering if my story was too much or not enough. I had gone from being a confident branding coach who helped others be seen to feeling small and unsure of how to show up myself.

I began to understand that sometimes God quiets us not to erase us, but to help us hear Him more clearly.

The ticking clock was no longer my enemy. It was my ally. Every delay, every quiet season, was teaching me patience, perspective, and preparation.

And when I finally spoke again, literally and figuratively, I wanted those words to mean something. Not to fill space or impress, but to serve.

Because the biggest freedom you can give yourself is to stop making excuses, placing blame, or being the victim. Take ownership in every area of your life. That ownership is where courage begins.

That silence did not steal my voice; it helped me find the strength behind it.

There were other seasons when I had felt that same restlessness, bouncing from one idea to the next, chasing clarity but never quite finding peace about business, homeschooling, or my health. Eventually, I reached a point where I knew something had to change. The summer before I got sick, just before turning fifty, I finally got serious about my wellbeing and was in the best shape I had been in a decade. It reminded me that nothing changes until you decide to change.

Healing, progress, and purpose all require participation.

Because I had been there.

I knew what it felt like to be stuck in survival, to lose sight of yourself, to feel like "enough" was behind you.

But God does not leave us there.

He strengthens us quietly, preparing us for what is next.

If He had given me all the answers before my body and spirit were ready, I would not have been able to carry them.

Patience was not punishment. It was preparation.

In many ways, it reminded me of tulips. Their quiet elegance, their strength disguised as simplicity. They do not bloom through chaos; they wait for the right season, pushing through the cold earth with quiet determination. Healing felt a lot like that. Unseen for a while. Then, when the time was right, new life broke through, simple, steady, and strong.

The Mission Defined

Looking back, I can see the golden thread that runs through everything I have ever done, from fashion blogger to branding coach to speaker and founder of Tough Like Tammy.

That thread was never just about business or image. It was about helping women see themselves again. Whether I was styling an outfit, building a brand, or now standing on a stage, the work was always the same at its core: helping women remember who they are and reflect that truth with confidence.

It has never really been about being seen by the world. It is about being seen by yourself again, the woman God created you to be before the world told you who you had to become.

Because when a woman finally sees herself clearly, she finds her voice.

And when she uses that voice to share her story, she creates impact far beyond what she can see.

Maybe that happens from a stage.

Maybe it happens around a kitchen table, or during a quiet morning drive, or in the mirror when you finally look yourself in the eye and say, "I am still here."

My mission now is simple but powerful:

To help women rediscover who they are, believe in what they carry, and have the courage to use it.

To help them share their stories and use their voices to impact others.

To remind them that they are capable of more than survival.

That their strength is not in striving. It is in surrendering.

And that the same God who carried me through my valley is faithful to walk them through theirs.

Because when a woman remembers her worth, uses her voice, and shares her story, the whole world around her begins to heal.

When life shifts, do not resist it. Lean in.

Embrace your life pivots, for within them lies the power to transform, to rise, and to thrive.

Reflection for You

Growth rarely happens all at once. It is a collection of small obediences, a thousand quiet yeses when no one is watching.

- Where might you be overcomplicating what God is asking you to do?
- What pressure could you release to make space for peace?
- What golden thread has been woven through your own story all along?

Your mission doesn't have to look big to make an impact.
It just has to look like obedience.

CHAPTER 10

The Space Between Strength and Surrender

The morning light slipped through the blinds in thin, golden stripes that fell across my desk. The dogs were curled up nearby, content and snoring softly, while my coffee had already cooled beside the laptop I had not opened yet. Notifications blinked on my phone like small, impatient hands waving for attention.

A few days earlier, I had been under the bright lights of a stage, sharing my story with a room full of women who had come hungry for hope. The energy, the faces, the presence of God in that space filled me to overflowing. Now I was home, surrounded by the ordinary things that made up my life: emails, laundry, client work, and a grocery list scribbled on a sticky note.

I had prayed for this season, for open doors, for a platform, for opportunities to share truth and light. But opportunity, I was learning, comes carrying its own to-do list.

That familiar ache started behind my eyes, the one that usually means I have pushed too hard for too long. It crept down into my shoulders, that old signal that it was time to pause. I pressed the pressure points above my brows, hoping to ease the tension. "Not today," I muttered. "There is too much to do."

I knew screen time did not help, but the deadlines were waiting: a virtual keynote in two weeks, the first draft of this book due by the end of the month, and client projects that could not be delayed. I never missed a physical therapy session, but anything beyond that, getting to the gym or exercising at home, just was not happening.

Then there were the emotional things. Our daughter was celebrating her first birthday away from home as a college student, so I was packaging up a box filled with confetti, baked cupcakes, and little notes, wanting her to feel wrapped in love across the miles. At the same time, our eighteen-year-old chihuahua was nearing the end of his life, and we were having those tender, heartbreaking conversations about when to let him go. In addition, there was the planning of an upcoming family trip, and all the organization required to prepare and get out the door, which felt like a full-time job in itself. I was also trying to stay present for my husband, who still deserved my full attention when I finally closed the laptop each night. It felt like everything good and everything hard was happening all at once.

It was not that I was ungrateful, far from it. I was in awe of how far God had brought me. But even gratitude can feel heavy when it is piled high with responsibility. I realized that morning that I was living in the space between answered prayer and quiet obedience, between strength and surrender.

I got down on the floor to stretch, taking a few deep breaths until my spine eased and the tension softened. As I leaned forward, I whispered a short prayer, half plea and half confession.

"Lord, help me slow down before something forces me to."

I could almost feel His answer, not in words, but in that familiar nudge toward peace. So I made a small promise to myself: I would focus on one thing at a time. I would stop measuring the day by how much I produced and start noticing how present I felt while doing it.

It sounded simple. It never was.

All month, I kept having to remind myself of that plan. Some days I succeeded. Some days I failed miserably. There were moments I felt unstoppable, fueled by purpose and the excitement of new doors opening. Then there were afternoons when the thought of another Zoom call made me want to crawl under a blanket and hide from my own ambition.

That tension, between gratitude and exhaustion, became my teacher.

I started to notice that the drive to do more was not always divinely led. Sometimes it was fear dressed up as purpose. Fear that if I did not keep moving, the opportunities would disappear. Fear that if I rested, people would forget me. Fear that I might disappoint the God who had carried me this far.

But God does not demand burnout as proof of faithfulness. He invites partnership.

One afternoon, as I sat outside listening to the birds and soaking in the sun, He reminded me of the verse that has carried me through every high and low:

"I can do all things through Christ who gives me strength."
Philippians 4:13

I had repeated those words countless times before, usually as a pep talk to push through something hard. But that day they landed differently. The emphasis shifted. Through Christ, not through sheer willpower, not through caffeine, not through overbooking myself to prove I was capable. Strength was not about how much I could hold. It was about Who was holding me.

That realization softened something in me. I stopped trying to juggle everything at once and began to ask, What has God actually asked me to carry today? Not the whole month, not every expectation, just today.

And when I approached the day that way, peace began to slip back in. I noticed the light again. I heard the sound of coffee pouring from the pot, the simple comfort of my morning routine. I caught myself smiling.

For a long time, I believed resilience meant endurance, grit your teeth, push through, keep climbing. But maybe real resilience is discernment: knowing when to rest, when to release, and when to let God move instead of you.

That thought became my quiet mantra through the rest of the month. Whenever the tension built behind my eyes or my chest tightened with overwhelm, I would whisper, "One thing at a time." It did not erase the work or the deadlines, but it returned me to the present moment, where grace lives.

I decided to take a real break. I logged off social media and silenced my notifications. The world didn't end. My business didn't crumble. What happened instead was stillness.

Larry poured the morning coffee while sunlight stretched across the back yard. For once, I wasn't already halfway through my mental checklist. I just sat there, listening to the gentle pour and feeling gratitude sink deeper than usual.

That day became a reset. I rested, laughed with Larry, spoke with Montana to hear every detail about her week, and enjoyed the sound of Nick and our grandson, Grayson, laughing together. I felt like myself again, steady, present, grateful.

Another time I experienced that same kind of reset came in the form of a girls' trip to Hawaii with my dear friends, Erica and Ameris. It was the biggest gift of love, complete with new confidence-building experiences and endless laughter. I knew how much work it would be for them, pushing my wheelchair through airports, helping me to the airplane bathroom (their can-do attitude made an awkward situation laughable), even giving me piggyback rides down to the water's edge.

We laughed the entire trip. The air smelled like salt and hibiscus, and for the first time in a long time, I felt the rhythm of waves instead of machines. One night before heading home, I went to a rock concert with their friend Julee, who lived on the island. We sat up close in the ADA section, an incredible view with the perfect blend of sound and energy. I could feel the beat of the music vibrating through my body as the crowd sang along, thousands of voices rising together. For a while, I forgot about everything else and just joined in, laughing, singing, living.

Afterward, Julee and I could not stop talking about the show, replaying our favorite songs and moments as we drove back through the warm Hawaiian night. The whole evening felt alive, a reminder of what it means to be part of something bigger than yourself.

The trip was full of laughter, friendship, and freedom, the kind of moments that remind you that life can still surprise you with joy.

I came home lighter. The trip reminded me that joy does not erase the hard parts of our stories; it gives them balance.

It struck me how much I had confused peace with passivity. I used to think slowing down meant losing ground. But what if peace is actually the strategy? What if rest is the soil where purpose grows?

When I stopped forcing momentum, God started showing me which doors were really mine to walk through and which ones were distractions dressed as opportunities.

That's the thing about surrender: it isn't giving up; it's giving *over*. It's trusting that the same God who opened the door will also tell you when to close it.

Success started to look different after that. It wasn't the number of followers or emails answered, the stage invitations or deadlines met. It was the mornings when I felt joy rising instead of pressure. It was being able to say no without guilt, to choose alignment over applause.

I realized that editing my life was not just about cutting out what was bad; it was about curating what was true.

Every time I slowed down enough to ask, "God, what do You want this to look like?" the answer was not more effort, it was more trust.

Maybe that is what maturity looks like in faith: not chasing every calling at once but learning to walk, step by step, in the rhythm of grace.

And when you find that rhythm, you stop performing for peace and start living from it.

That is what this chapter is really about, the meaningful middle space between strength and surrender. The place where you no longer have to prove your worth because you finally understand Who gives it to you.

Reflection for You

Maybe you are in that same space right now, the one where the dreams you prayed for have arrived, but they come with responsibilities that stretch you thin. Where gratitude and exhaustion coexist.

Pause and ask yourself:

- What has God actually asked me to carry today?
- Where am I striving from fear instead of flowing from faith?
- What would it look like to trust His timing, even if it means slowing down?

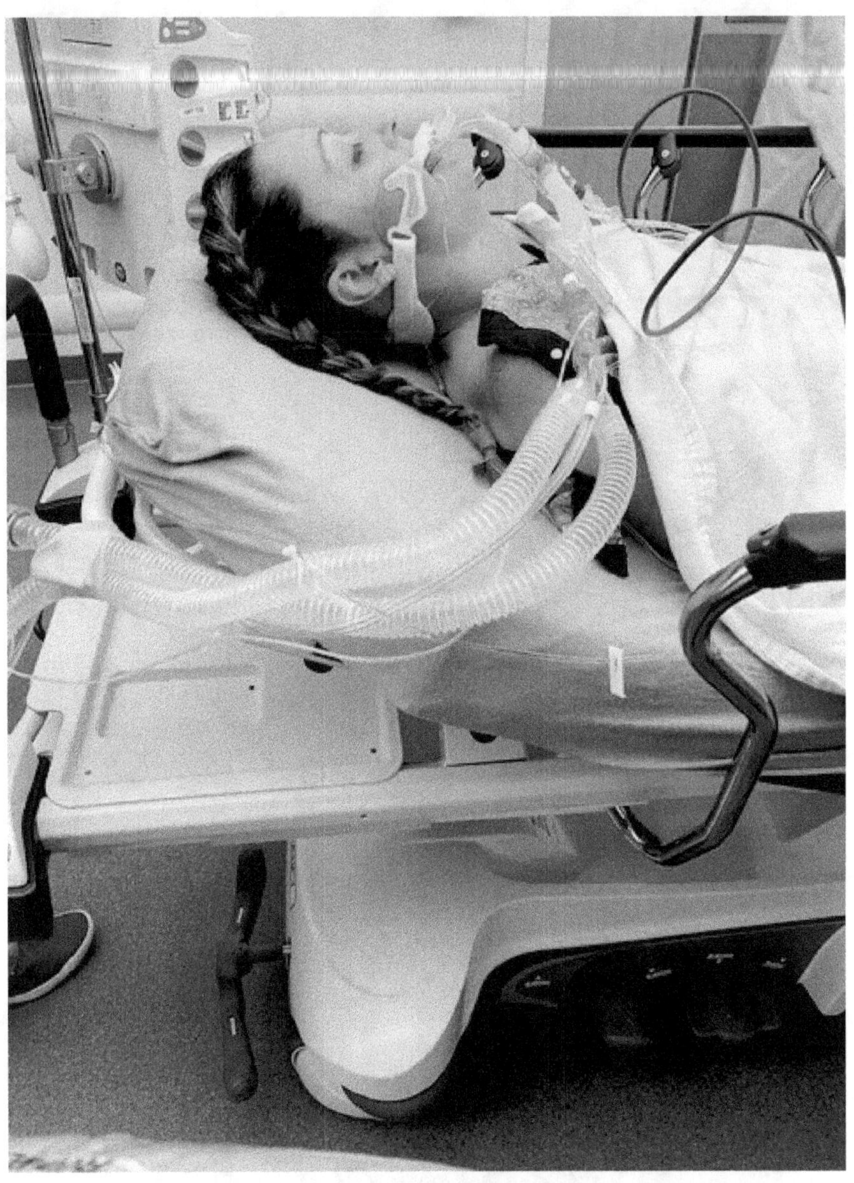

Oct 2021 *Two days in, still fighting for breath and
for another chance at life.*

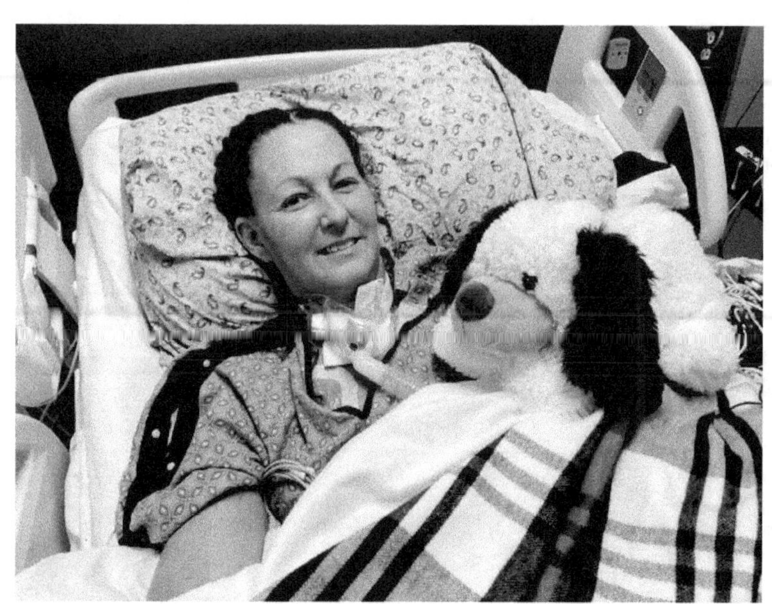

December 2021-Hope returning, one smile at a time.

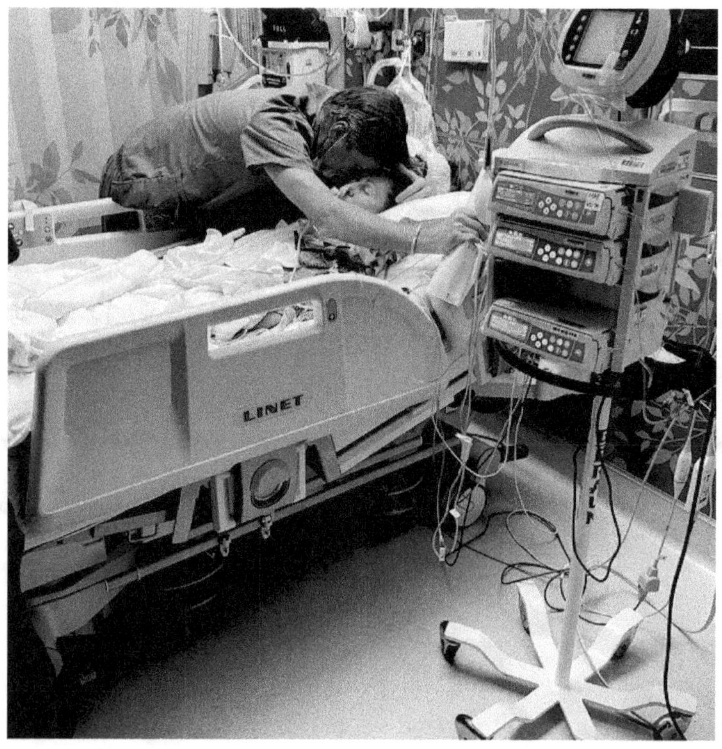

Love that refused to leave the room.

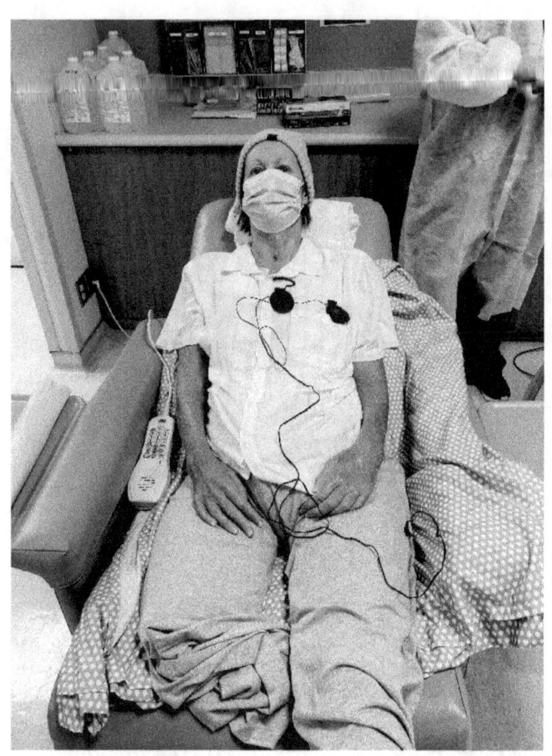

March 2022- Outpatient dialysis: numb, sick, but still showing up.

Outpatient Physical Therapy Dream Team

The moment movement felt like me again.

*God gave us friendship and the kind of laughter that heals
from the inside out.*

Dec 2022- Last Christmas, a hospital room.
This year, home, surrounded by love.

April 2022- Two months home, carried by grace and the love of my parents every step of the way.

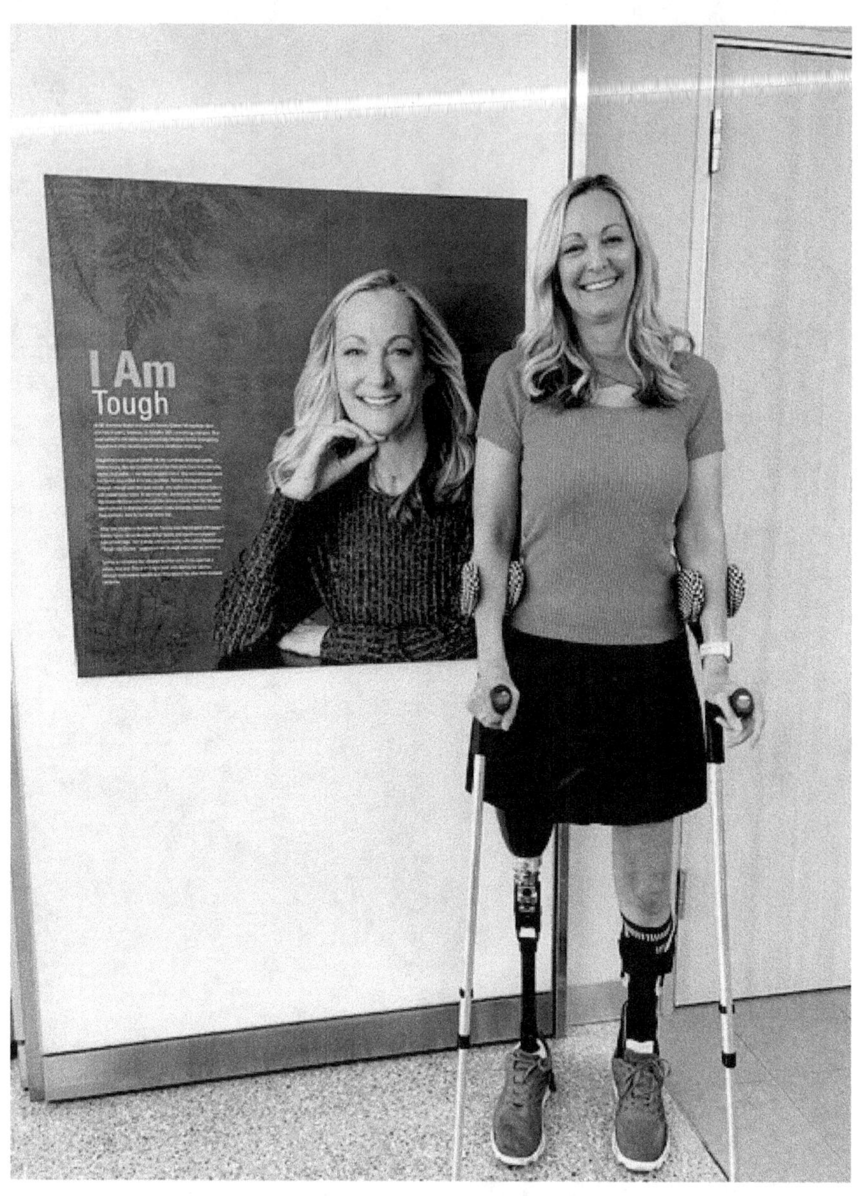

*Sept 2025- From hospital bed to hallway wall,
proof that God's not finished yet.*

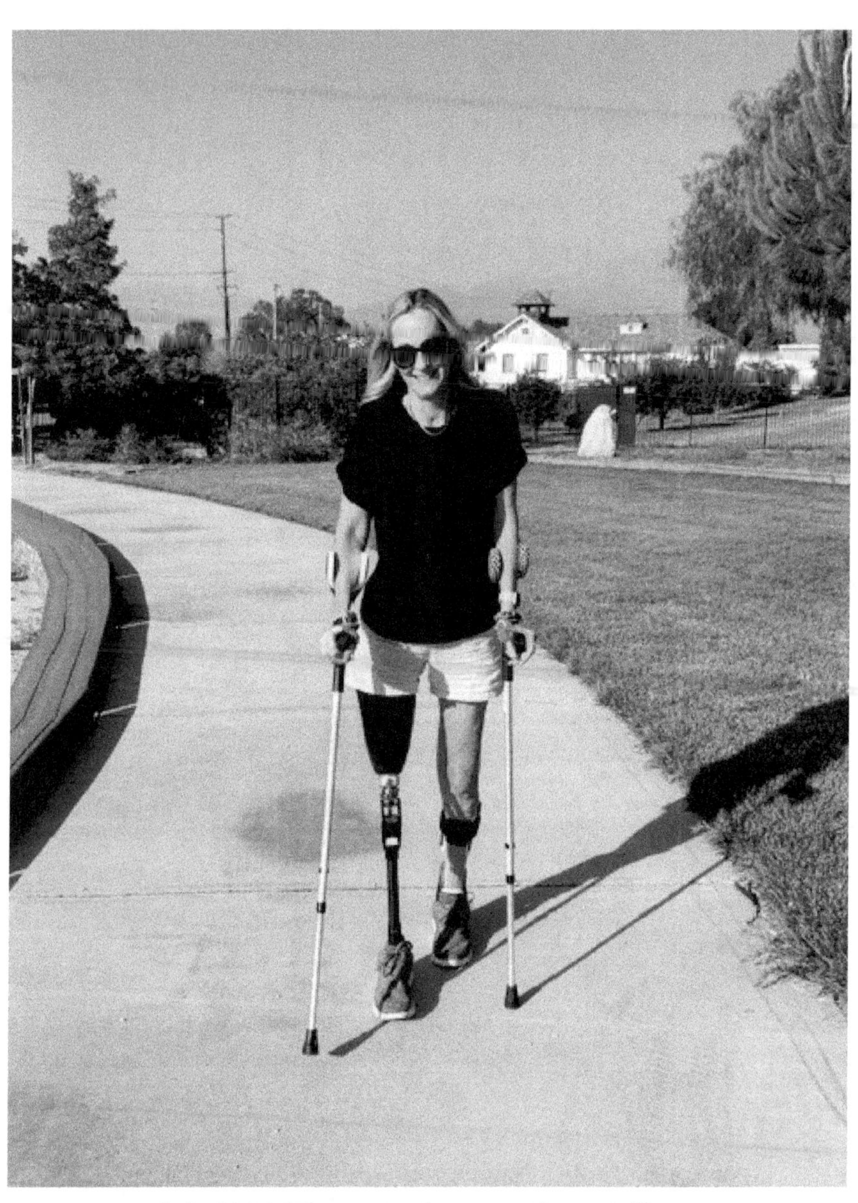

*July 2025- Three years later- smiling, walking,
and grateful for every step.*

Once silenced by sickness, now speaking life and hope into others.

CHAPTER 11

The Comeback Edit – Rewriting the Story You Tell Yourself

The hum of my laptop was the only sound in the room. On the screen, a short video from a recent event played on loop, me speaking, laughing, gesturing, a crowd leaning in. I dragged the brightness slider up a little, softened the shadows, and trimmed the clip so the awkward pause at the beginning disappeared. One click smoothed everything out.

Editing had always been part of my world. Back when I blogged about fashion, I could spend an hour adjusting one photo, fixing lighting, cropping clutter, toning down a color that pulled too much attention. I was not trying to fake perfection; I just wanted the image to reflect how it felt in the moment. Still, that afternoon as I worked through the footage, I caught myself wondering: how many of us are still doing that, editing our lives not to capture truth, but to control the narrative?

The irony hit me. I had spent years building a career around visibility, yet I was realizing that some of the most important edits in life have nothing to do with appearance. They are the internal adjustments we make when we realize the version of ourselves we have been showing the world no longer fits.

That is what this chapter is about, learning to edit from the inside out.

I call it **The Comeback Edit** because it is not just about changing what is on the surface. It is about returning to life, to joy, to yourself, and to the purpose God planted in you long before the pressure began. It is that moment when you realize, *I am back, baby!* Full of life, inspired, hopeful, and most importantly, moving forward.

I paused the video and stared at the still frame. The woman on the screen looked confident, animated, and alive. But what the camera could not see were the moments between events, the quiet doubts, the mental clutter, the internal conversations where I questioned whether I was still walking in alignment or just keeping up appearances. Those were the spaces where God kept whispering, "You do not have to perform for Me, just be who I created you to be."

In the world of social media, we are conditioned to believe that editing is about making things look better. Brighten the colors. Sharpen the edges. Cut what feels too slow. But true editing, the kind that changes your life, is about clarity, not cosmetics. It is about deciding what no longer belongs in the frame.

I used to think transformation came from adding more effort, more discipline, more goals. But editing taught me that growth often happens through subtraction. When we start removing the noise, what remains is what is true, and what is true always brings us closer to the voice of peace that has been guiding us all along.

I did not always recognize it that way. For a long time, I clung to the version of myself that got me through survival mode, the woman who could push through anything. She was strong, capable, and productive. But she also had a hard time slowing down long enough to ask if all that striving was still necessary. Eventually, I realized that even strength without surrender can keep you from hearing God's direction.

That is the tricky thing about healing and success. Both can become new kinds of armor. You start protecting yourself with accomplishments instead of fear. You stay busy so you will not have to feel uncertain. And slowly, without realizing it, you begin performing a story that is not fully yours anymore.

The first time I really understood this was when I watched one of my own interviews back. I had just answered a question about resilience, and my words sounded fine, honest, hopeful, but something about my expression caught me. My smile looked a little tired, like my spirit was half a step behind my voice.

That moment stayed with me, I realized editing is not about erasing the past; it is about revealing what is real right now. It is the pause between what was and what is next, the decision point where you ask, *Does this still represent who I am growing into?* And for me, that question often becomes a prayer: "Lord, help me see what You see."

That question became my quiet compass. Whenever life started to feel out of focus, too busy, too noisy, too heavy, I would remind myself: *Maybe it is time for another comeback edit.*

For me, The Comeback Edit was not about image management anymore. It was about alignment, making sure the story I was telling with my life actually matched the truth of my heart and the calling God placed within it.

And here is the thing about truth: it is rarely loud. It does not shout or demand attention. It sits patiently beneath the surface, waiting for us to slow down long enough to listen. That stillness has become, for me, the place where I meet God most clearly.

Over time, I realized that the process of editing, whether it is a photo, a project, or a personal narrative, always follows a rhythm. You do not just delete what is wrong; you observe, evaluate, refine, and rebuild. You make peace with imperfection while choosing what matters most.

That rhythm became the framework for how I live and lead today. It is the same process that shaped my recovery, my career, and my faith, the blueprint I use to align my external world with my internal truth.

Each step invites a new layer of honesty and courage. It is not a one-time fix; it is a lifelong practice of curating a life that reflects who you really are, not who you think you need to be.

In the next section, I will walk you through the four core movements of The Comeback Edit: Pause, Reflect, Refine, and Rebuild. But before you start learning the steps, take a deep breath and remember this: editing your life is not about perfection. It is about peace, presence, and trusting the One who is guiding your comeback.

Pause

The first step in any comeback is learning to pause.

After years of momentum, stillness can feel unnatural, like braking too hard after a long run. Yet every meaningful edit begins there.

Before I got sick, Pilates was my pause. I had grown fond of it the summer before everything changed. Three or four times a week, I would walk into class, slip off my shoes, and let the rhythm of movement quiet my mind. It was my favorite time of day, a space where strength and stillness met. For that hour, I was not thinking about business or deadlines or what needed to be done. I was fully present in my body.

After coming home from the hospital, I was not sure I would ever feel that kind of connection again. But slowly, with my favorite instructor, Lupe, guiding me through gentle movements, I began to rebuild trust with my body. She reminded me to breathe, to move with intention, to celebrate small victories, an extra lift, a deeper stretch, a moment of balance I had not had before.

Pilates became more than exercise. It was a restorative kind of stillness, the place where I learned that pause is not just rest; it is awareness. It is the breath between what was and what is next.

That pause did not fix everything overnight, but it created room to breathe, and room is where truth begins to surface. Pausing is not quitting; it is noticing. It is stepping back far enough to see what is really in the frame.

Takeaway: When life starts to blur, stop pushing. Find your pause, the space that brings you back to yourself. That is where the comeback begins.

Reflect

Once you pause, reflection follows naturally. It is the review stage, the moment you look at your raw footage and ask, What am I really seeing?

During my recovery, reflection looked like simple questions captured in the Notes app on my phone:

Is this habit helping me heal or keeping me stuck?
Do I still want what I used to want?
What would alignment look like today?

Reflection isn't about judgment; it's about curiosity. It asks us to tell the truth without dramatizing it. Just facts, feelings, and gentle honesty.

But sometimes, the hardest part of reflection isn't what we see, it's what we refuse to see. The stories we cling to because they make us feel safe. The labels we wear because they've defined us for so long. The pain we avoid because naming it means we might have to change something.

For me, that often looked like overexplaining my exhaustion or brushing off the signals my body was giving me. It was easier to keep moving than to face what slowing down might reveal. But until I admitted those truths, I couldn't rewrite them.

Takeaway: Reflection is the bridge between awareness and change. You can't edit what you refuse to see—and you can't heal what you keep hiding.

Refine

After reflection comes refinement, the courageous part. This is where you trim, crop, and rebalance the story. You start removing what does not serve your next season.

For the first year of recovery, physical therapy, neuropathic therapy, and occupational therapy were my priorities. Some weeks, I had six or more appointments. As I got stronger, I realized I had so many tools I could use on my own that I didn't need as many sessions. I could do my therapy at home or at Citrus Valley PT, where I was already working out.

That decision was refinement in action. It cut the unnecessary busyness from my schedule and gave me breathing room again. If I hadn't refined that part of my routine, I might have stayed stuck in the cycle of overdoing—mistaking busyness for progress. Refining my schedule allowed me to focus on what was actually most effective for my healing and strength.

Refinement isn't punishment; it's precision. It's choosing excellence over excess. Each adjustment creates space for what matters most.

Takeaway: Every "no" becomes a stronger "yes." Refinement is how peace takes shape.

Rebuild

Rebuilding is the final and ongoing movement of the comeback. It is where vision meets action again, but from a new center of gravity.

I think of the first time I rolled up in front of an audience after my amputation. I was not the same woman who had once thrived on how many activities she could fit into a day. I was steadier. Slower. More intentional. That moment wasn't about proving anything; it was about honoring who I am in this chapter.

Rebuilding is where confidence and clarity meet. It is waking up each day and choosing to live as the edited version of yourself, aware, aligned, and alive. It is trusting that what was removed was not wasted; it made room for what is next.

Takeaway: A true comeback isn't about restoring the past; it's about honoring the edits that life has made and choosing to build from here.

Reflection for You

Comebacks don't happen in one grand moment, they unfold through steady, intentional edits. Each small adjustment becomes a declaration that you're choosing peace over perfection, alignment over appearance.

- Where do you sense it's time to pause before you press forward?
- What truth have you been avoiding that might actually set you free?
- Which habits or expectations could you refine to create more space for peace and progress?
- How might you rebuild your days, not to prove you're back, but to honor the woman you've become?

Your comeback doesn't require permission.

It just requires presence.

CHAPTER 12

Grace Under Pressure

The drive to Newport Beach felt like possibility.

Larry and I wound down the freeway, the sun shining through the windows just enough for the warm May day to shine through. My long purple tulle skirt rested carefully across my lap, part confidence and part armor. It was the first business event I'd attended since getting sick, and I was determined to show up as the woman I still believed myself to be.

Before I entered into that workshop, I had been doing a lot of reflecting on the idea of giving myself grace. It is a phrase we hear everywhere, usually wrapped in softness and self-compassion, and for good reason. Grace is essential. Grace keeps us gentle with ourselves when life demands more than we have. Grace gives us room to breathe when the world feels tight.

But there is a difference between giving yourself grace and quietly staying stuck.

For months I told myself I was taking my time when the truth was that I was afraid to move forward. I confused slowness with safety. I confused pausing with hiding. I confused grace with avoidance. And when you blur those lines long enough, you can convince yourself that inaction is healing when it is actually hesitation.

Grace is meant to support your movement, not replace it.

Healthy grace sounds like: I am human. I am healing. I am growing at a pace that honors my body and my spirit.

Stuckness sounds like: I will start when I feel ready. I need more clarity before I take the next step. I do not want to try until I can do it perfectly. I will move forward when things calm down.

One is compassionate.
The other is protective.

One creates space
The other creates delay.

Real grace is active. It gently ushers you forward even when you are scared. Stuckness convinces you to wait for a moment that may never come.

Over time I realized that the difference is not in the pace but in the posture. You can move slowly and still be moving. You can take your time and still be walking your path. But when the pause becomes a pattern, when the quiet becomes longer than the growth, that is when grace needs to shift into courage.

That workshop became a turning point because it forced me to confront that distinction. I was still learning what it meant to show up before I felt polished. To be visible before I felt confident. To take my next step without waiting for the perfect moment to appear.

Grace is what softened me enough to roll into that room. Courage is what kept me there. And honesty is what helped me see the difference between the two.

The workshop was held at a yacht club overlooking the water. Bright, open, and minimalist, it was the kind of space that seemed to exhale calm. White linens covered round tables.

High-energy music pulsed through the speakers, the kind that makes you straighten your posture and smile without realizing it. Boats glided past the tall windows behind the tables we sat at, sunlight dancing across their wakes. The air smelled faintly of the host's perfume, sophisticated and warm, just like her.

I'd followed Emily online for years. I admired her glam-meets-grit style, her bold faith, her kindness. And now, here I was in a room of thirty women, each impeccably dressed, skin glowing, heels clicking, hair cascading past their shoulders, while I sat in my chair with my brace visible beneath layers of soft fabric.

I was nervous, yes, but also thrilled. For the first time in a long time, my mind felt alive again, buzzing with creative energy and ideas. During the breaks, I chatted with the women at my table, exchanging stories and laughter. When the host called for a dance break, the room erupted with movement. I joined in from my chair, swaying, clapping, letting joy move through me anyway.

But on the first day, when it was my turn to share, something shifted.

We'd been asked to describe our ideal brand and how it reflected who we are. I spoke honestly, maybe too honestly, about the tension I felt between the image in my head and the woman in the mirror.

"I love elegant, editorial style with a touch of glam and edginess," I said, my voice catching. "But lately, I've struggled with what to wear for this new body. I don't even know how to show up online when my own image feels like it's still under construction."

Tears came before I could stop them. The kind that rises from deep within your chest and betrays the composure you wanted to hold. I felt the room go quiet. Every insecurity I'd been wrestling with, visibility, confidence, identity, seemed to echo through that silence.

That night, back at the hotel, Larry ordered room service and we ate dinner in bed, salads and fries, our version of balance. We laughed about little things, but my mind kept replaying the moment I cried. I wondered if I'd said too much. If my vulnerability looked like weakness.

The next morning, as I wheeled into the room, Emily met me with a hug. "I just have to tell you," she said, "I thought you were the most elegant woman in the room yesterday. You showed up when you could have stayed home. You're chasing your dreams when most people would still be trying to accept their new normal."

Her words landed like light through glass, gentle, clear, illuminating.

Grace.

That moment changed how I saw myself. I realized the image I held in my mind, frail, in progress, messy in the middle, wasn't what others saw. They saw courage. They saw presence.

They saw a woman still in the process but willing to show up anyway.

Grace under pressure, I learned, isn't about holding it all together. It's about being honest enough to admit that you don't have to. It's the art of allowing imperfection to coexist with progress.

That weekend reminded me that we all have messy middles. The gap between who we were and who we're growing into can feel awkward and uncertain, but that's where transformation happens. The real strength is in showing up during the edit, not after it's complete.

The rest of the workshop was a blur of laughter, learning, and quiet confidence. I left lighter—not because the pressure was gone, but because grace had made space within it.

The truth is, grace doesn't remove the challenge; it redefines it. It invites us to keep moving forward without losing ourselves in the process.

Living with Grace in Motion

Grace under pressure isn't a single moment, it's a rhythm you learn to live by.

It's the choice to stay soft in a world that rewards hard edges, to stay steady when everything around you moves faster than your spirit wants to go.

After the Newport workshop, I started paying closer attention to the small ways I could make space for grace in my daily life. I realized that the same patience I needed in recovery was the patience I now needed in rebuilding my career and confidence. Grace, I learned, doesn't just get you through the hard seasons—it teaches you how to live when the pace picks back up.

1. *Slow Starts, Strong Days*

These days, grace looks like beginning my mornings unrushed. I wake up early (for me!), not to get ahead but to ease in. There's something peaceful about those quiet minutes before the day begins: the sound of coffee pouring, the soft light through the blinds, the simple act of getting ready with intention instead of urgency.

For so long, I treated mornings as a countdown. Now they're my anchor. I don't open my messages until I've centered myself. I choose calm first, then I step into action. Grace reminds me that how I begin shapes how I move through everything that follows.

2. *Releasing the Timeline*

For most of my life, I believed that success had an expiration date, that healing, walking, writing a book, or building a brand should happen faster. I was always chasing the next milestone, convinced that progress meant pace.

But I've learned that grace doesn't rush. It trusts.

Every meaningful thing, including healing, clarity, and growth, takes time.

The world moves fast, but true transformation rarely does. Letting go of "when" has been one of the most freeing acts of faith I've ever practiced.

3. *Honest Friendships*

There are a few special friends I can text when I'm teetering between overwhelm and laughter. We take turns venting, encouraging, and holding space for one another. On good weeks, we're each other's cheerleaders. On tough ones, we're mutual lifelines.

It's comforting to know that grace often shows up through people, those who remind us we're not alone, who let us be real without needing to fix us. They help carry the emotional load when pressure tries to tip the scale.

4. *Everyday Conversations with God*

Grace, for me, is also an ongoing dialogue. I talk to God throughout the day, between tasks, during drives, even while folding laundry. It's less about structure and more about awareness, staying open to the quiet nudges that guide me.

When I listen, life flows smoother. When I ignore those small divine prompts, what others might call intuition, I almost always wish I hadn't. Grace is in that awareness too, the humility to pause, listen, and try again next time.

Music plays a big part in that connection. I keep songs playing most of the day, shifting the energy in the room as my mood or focus changes. Each song becomes a reset, a reminder that even under pressure, life can feel light.

Grace in Practice

Living with grace under pressure isn't about being calm all the time; it's about *choosing calm* when it would be easier to react. Over the past few years, I've learned that most situations don't need an immediate answer, they just need space.

I've become much better at not reacting. People love to toss ideas around, dream out loud, and move on to the next thing. Opportunities appear, plans shift, excitement builds and fades. If I jumped at every spark, I'd live in a constant state of motion and disappointment. So now, I let things breathe. I let conversations and circumstances play out. If something's meant for me, it doesn't need to be chased; it will keep showing up.

Grace gives me permission to pause before I respond. Whether it's an email, an invitation, or a curveball, I remind myself to hand it over and breathe. Give it room. Let the truth rise to the surface before the emotion takes over.

Twice now, while giving speeches, I planned to use a headset mic so I could move freely in my wheelchair—it would allow me to push with both hands and roll naturally. And twice, the headset wasn't available due to last-minute tech issues. I could've let frustration distract me. Instead, I smiled and said, "No problem! I'll use the handheld." I joked that pushing with one hand would just send me in a circle. Everyone laughed, and the moment loosened the room. It reminded me that grace isn't about perfect conditions; it's about showing up anyway.

I've also learned that grace applies to the things we *want* just as much as the things we fear. There was a speaking contest I had my eye on, eight minutes, virtual stage, and the prize was taking the stage at an in-person event with an audience of women eager to transform their lives, my ideal audience. I spent too much time debating whether to do it. The opportunity sounded exciting, but I had other commitments, and something inside me said, not this time. I finally surrendered, trusting that if it was meant to be, it would return. Saying no felt strangely peaceful, obedience wrapped in calm. Not every open door is an invitation. Sometimes grace says, bless and release.

Grace doesn't remove the desire to grow or succeed. It just realigns it. I still have goals, dreams, and a vision for the next season of my life. I simply hold them with open hands now. I've seen how God works when I stop forcing things. His timing is always kinder than mine.

When we learn to stop reacting, when we let life settle before we step in, we save ourselves from unnecessary stress, worry, and regret. Grace reminds us that our job isn't to control every outcome, it is to stay faithful in the process.

So, whether it's a tech mishap, a delayed opportunity, or a conversation that doesn't unfold as planned, I remind myself: Let Go and Let God. He sees what I can't. My role is to show up, stay steady, and trust the timing.

Grace isn't passive. It's power under control, the quiet confidence that comes from knowing you're held even when things don't go as planned.

Reflection for You

Pressure doesn't always leave when life gets better. It just changes form. Grace helps you move through it without losing your peace, your presence, or your joy.

- Where do you feel pressure showing up in your life right now?
- What expectation could you release to create more space for grace?

- Who has been a vessel of grace for you lately and how can you extend that same kindness to yourself?
- What does living with grace under pressure look like for you today, not in theory but in action?

You don't have to wait for calm to feel peaceful.
You can carry grace with you into the noise.

CHAPTER 13

The Comeback Lifestyle – Living Within the Reality Loop

It was one of those mornings that felt full of hope. We drove a couple of hours to a beachside mobility clinic where I thought I would finally get to try a running blade. The idea of moving freely again, even for a few steps, felt like magic. At that point, I was still using my walker full-time and had never walked on uneven ground, but I was determined to give it everything I had.

When we arrived, I quickly learned the setup was not what I had imagined. The sessions were being held on grass, and the running blades were not available for demo. You had to bring your own. My heart sank. I watched the other amputees line up for drills, most of them far more advanced than I was, and for a moment I felt like I did not belong there.

When I stepped into line, the instructor glanced at me, pulled me aside and said, matter of factly, that the group would not be waiting for me and that I could go at my own pace because the event was not designed for my level of mobility. I understood what he meant, but it still stung. I had come looking for inspiration and possibility. Instead, I felt small, embarrassed, and disappointed, mostly in myself.

I felt disappointed because I believed I should have been further along by then, as if more effort, more grit, more pushing should have automatically placed me among the advanced amputees lining up with ease. I felt disappointed because I had built up an expectation in my mind without ever asking what the event included. I assumed there would be running blades. I assumed the environment would meet me where I was. I assumed

I would walk into a moment that felt cinematic and affirming. And I know better than to assume. Truly. Yet there I was, doing exactly that.

When reality did not match the picture I had painted, it felt like a personal failure rather than a simple misunderstanding.

But the deepest disappointment was this: Why did a stranger's tone have the power to shrink me? Why did his matter of fact assessment of my mobility feel like a verdict on my worth? Why did I let his words sting so deeply that tears rose to my eyes? It was not really about him. It was about the part of me that was already tender, the part that wondered if I was too slow, too behind, too not there yet to belong. That, more than the grass, more than the missing blade, more than the setup, was the real ache of the moment.

My friend and prosthetist, Mike, was there, along with Larry. They encouraged me to take it one step at a time, literally and emotionally. I had wanted the day to feel exciting and empowering, but it felt like another reminder of how far I still had to go.

When Stuckness Comes From Inside

Before I continue the story, I want to pause here, because there is something important about this moment that every woman who feels stuck needs to understand. I was disappointed, but underneath that, I was stuck. Deeply stuck. Not physically. Emotionally.

There is a specific kind of stuckness we feel when we know we are meant for more but cannot seem to move toward it. It is not laziness or lack of desire. It is not a matter of trying harder. It is a tug-of-war between two truths: I want to grow and I do not know how to start.

Inside, stuckness sounds like this: I should be further along by now. Why can't I make progress? What is wrong with me? Why does this seem easier for everyone else?

I knew those thoughts well. Some days they were louder than any physical challenge I faced.

For years, I tried to fix that stuck feeling by forcing my thoughts into positivity. I repeated affirmations. I tried to think better. I tried to use my mindset to bulldoze my way into clarity. But nothing stuck, because I was starting in the wrong place. I was treating the symptoms, not the source.

That morning on the grass, I finally saw the root. I was not stuck because I lacked motivation or discipline. I was stuck because I was leading with the wrong emotion. Fear was leading. Comparison was leading. Frustration was leading. And when those emotions lead, your thoughts follow every time.

That moment became the first glimpse of what I now call the Reality Loop.

The Seed of the Reality Loop

At first, I felt the familiar trio: frustration, comparison, discouragement. My thoughts followed. I will never get there. Everyone here is ahead of me. Why did I even show up? That mindset made me want to give up before I started.

Then something shifted. I caught myself. I changed the question. Not why am I behind, but what do I want to feel right now?

The answer shifted something in me.

I wanted to feel proud, present, and grateful for progress. Not someday. Not when I reached a milestone. Not when life looked how I imagined. But now.

So I led with gratitude. "This is my first time walking on grass. This is progress."

Then I acted from that truth. I walked six laps across that field, about six hundred feet. It might not sound like much, but for me it was everything. By the end, I was sweaty, shaky, and proud. That single shift from frustration to gratitude changed the entire trajectory of the day.

I left with new confidence, new friends, and a clearer perspective. One person I met was an engineering PhD student working on a new above knee socket that was more functional and more stylish. We stayed in touch, and I later gave feedback on his design. I love knowing my perspective might help future amputees through the innovations he creates.

Looking back, I realize my hope for that day was not really about a running blade. It was about wanting to feel normal again, to move the way I used to. The truth was, I was not ready for that kind of speed yet. But I was ready for growth.

Everyday Lessons in Motion

A couple of years after that morning on the grass, I began to see that same awareness show up in the smallest places, even in the way I loaded my chair into the car. My progress had taken time, steady and slow, but it was still unfolding.

The garage was quiet except for the soft roll of my wheels over concrete, the creak of the hatch, the click of the walker as I set it beside the car. I lined myself up next to the back, took a breath, and eased myself onto the edge of the cargo space the way Heidi taught me. With the front casters lifted and my left hand steadying my balance, I used my right hand to guide the chair up and into the back of the car. It slid smoothly into place, and every time it happens like that, it still surprises me how natural the process has become.

I stood using the walker, eased the hatch down, then made my way to the driver's door. I removed my prosthetic because it is my right leg and gets in the way of the gas pedal, set it in the passenger seat, and settled in. Mirrors adjusted and engine running, I turned the music low and released a long breath I did not know I had been carrying.

Freedom does not always arrive with fireworks. Sometimes it shows up as a Tuesday drive to the gym, hard won, ordinary, and meaningful all at once. That first time I did it alone, I felt two emotions at the same time: joy and pride. Joy for the freedom. Pride for the independence. Those emotions shaped the thoughts that followed. "You are capable. You are growing. Keep going."

The Missing Piece in the Mindset Equation

This was when the pattern I had studied for years finally clicked. I had worked in personal development long enough to know the slogans: Change your thoughts, change your life. That never sat quite right with me.

I could change a sentence in my head and still feel stuck in my body. I could speak affirmations and still move through my day guarded by fear. Words alone were not moving the needle.

What finally made sense was realizing that my thoughts were not the starting point. My emotions were. And for the first time in years, I understood why I had felt so stuck. I had been trying to think my way into a feeling instead of feeling my way into movement.

"What do I want to feel?" Not someday. Not when the goal is reached. Not when life finally looks how I imagined. But now.

Because the feeling I longed for was not waiting on the other side of achievement. It was waiting on the other side of awareness.

When I began to notice how my emotions shaped my thoughts, which then shaped my actions, everything clicked into place. When I lead with fear, my thoughts become small. When I lead with gratitude, my thoughts widen. When I choose awe, my thoughts open the door to wonder, possibility, and courage. Awe is what I feel when God threads a miracle into an ordinary day. It amplifies trust. It makes room for hope.

Most people set goals based on tangibles, numbers, milestones, achievements. But what if the real goal is emotional? What if joy, peace, and gratitude are not rewards for reaching the finish line, but the path itself?

When we choose the emotion first, we experience the fulfillment we have been waiting for all along.

The Ten Second Reset

To make this practical, I use something I call the Ten Second Reset.

Notice what you feel.
Name it without judgment.
Choose the emotion you want to lead with next, such as gratitude, confidence, peace, or awe.
Act with one small step within thirty seconds.

You will feel the loop begin to move.

Reality Loop → Emotion → Thought → Action → Repeat

This is the flow I live by now. Emotion sets the tone. Thought gives meaning. Action makes it real. Then the result reinforces the original emotion, for better or worse, and the loop keeps spinning.

When I lead with stress, I think stressful thoughts, take frantic action, and create more stress. When I lead with positive emotions like gratitude, awe, compassion, and hope, my thoughts become creative and courageous. My actions follow, and my days reflect it.

Emotional Maturity: Feel It, Then Steward It

Living inside the Reality Loop does not mean letting emotions run the show. It means learning how to steward them. Maturity is not pretending you do not feel things. It is feeling fully and choosing wisely.

I practice it this way. Notice what I feel. Normalize it by remembering that feelings are data, not destiny. Narrow my focus by choosing the emotion I want to lead with next, even if another emotion lingers. Navigate by letting that leader emotion shape my next thought and next action. For example, if I feel overwhelmed before a meeting, I pause and name it. I remind myself that overwhelm is simply information, not a verdict. Then I choose calm or confidence to lead the moment. From that emotion, I take a breath, gather my notes, and begin. The entire experience shifts because the leader emotion shifted.

I also know that nervous and excited feel the same in the body. Before a speech, when I sense that flutter, I remind myself, "I am not nervous. I am excited." The physical sensation is the same, but the meaning I give it changes everything.

This is where the lesson from the previous chapter becomes real. Most things do not need an instant reply. Grace lives in the gap between the feeling and the action. I have learned to create that gap on purpose. Breathe. Pray. Let the wave pass. Then decide.

Being rooted in God's presence helps me hold that ground. I am not trying to control outcomes anymore. I am partnering with Him in how I respond.

A Day Made of Comebacks

My comeback is not a single scene. It is a day made of small edits. Transitioning from the walker to forearm crutches. Cooking dinner again after months away from the stove. Checking off one goal in physical therapy and celebrating the micro-win. Independently loading my chair and driving to the gym again and again until it felt natural.

None of those moments happened because I forced my thoughts to behave. They happened because I led with emotion on purpose, emotions like joy, trust, gratitude, and acceptance. Those emotions fueled thoughts like "You are the kind of woman who learns hard things. You can adjust. You can rest. You can repeat." Those thoughts made room for consistent action. The loop reinforced itself, and my reality began to mirror what I believed was possible.

When life gets loud, emotional order matters more than emotional control. I have learned that I do not have to silence my feelings to stay steady. I just have to decide which one gets to lead. When we ignore our feelings, we cannot heal. Emotional order is permission to feel paired with the wisdom to choose.

When the Loop Slips

Of course, I still slip. Fatigue creeps in. A plan changes. A comment lands wrong. And just like that, my loop starts to slide toward stress or comparison. The difference is that I notice it sooner now. Awareness has become my early warning system.

When I feel the sting, I name it. I let it cool. I choose again.

The goal is not to be unbothered. The goal is to stay anchored.

Emotion → Thought → Action (In Motion)

At the gym, I lead with pride in my independence. My thought becomes "You are the kind of woman who learns hard things." I drive myself, remember what I was taught in physical therapy, and move into my workout, strengthening my muscles and building endurance. I love watching my body grow stronger and seeing my muscles develop, and that motivates my actions too. It is not headline-worthy, but it is progress. That small loop of emotion, thought, and action ends in a quiet win that multiplies pride and joy.

Around the dinner table, gratitude leads the way. My thought becomes "These are my people. This is the life I prayed for." I cook something simple, linger longer, and listen more than I speak. Warmth rises, and gratitude doubles back. The way dinner tastes better when I cook it, though never quite as good as when Larry does.

When an unexpected email lands, peace leads. My thought becomes "I can respond tomorrow with clarity." I draft a note, save it, and sleep on it. By morning, the reply is calm and kind. What could have turned into stress dissolves instead.

Awareness does not erase frustration or fear. It gives you a choice in how to meet them.

Awe: My Favorite On-Ramp

If gratitude is my daily reset, awe is the spark that keeps life vibrant. Awe widens the frame. It turns ordinary moments into evidence of the extraordinary. Awe remembers how far I have come. Awe whispers

"Look what God can do with a life that refuses to quit." Awe transforms survival into celebration

I return to awe because it is how I move from surviving what happened to celebrating what is still possible.

When I lead with awe, joy does not wait for the finish line. It begins in the noticing: the stars scattered across the night sky, the sunrise that keeps showing up after every hard night, the laughter that breaks tension at the right moment, the way snowflakes form in perfect silence, the divine timing I could never orchestrate myself.

Each moment reminds me that God is here, that I am growing, and that life is still beautiful. Awe is quiet clarity. It steadies my heart when things feel uncertain.

Co-Creating With God

I have learned to expect miracles. I even have those words inked on my arm. Expecting miracles does not mean sitting still and waiting for life to happen to me. It means showing up, preparing, and trusting outcomes to God.

Pray like it depends on God. Work like it depends on you. This keeps me humble and hungry.

Control clutches. Co-creation trusts. Control demands a timeline. Co-creation honors timing. Control breaks under pressure. Co-creation bends with grace and stands when the storm passes.

Like a palm tree rooted deeply, flexible enough to move but not uprooted, that is how I want to live: anchored in faith, resilient in practice, open to divine timing.

Guardrails for a Comeback Lifestyle

Living within the Reality Loop is not about perfection. It is about rhythm.

I start my mornings slow. Coffee, sunlight, prayer, a quiet breath. On the best days, I do not touch messages until I am centered. Those minutes set the tone for everything that follows.

I move the body I have. Some days that means physical therapy. Other days it is stretching in my chair. Movement creates energy, and energy creates hope.

Before big tasks, I pause to choose a leader emotion. Gratitude. Awe. Peace. Confidence. That one choice determines how I show up.

I have learned the power of the pause. Not everything needs an instant reply. A deep breath and a whispered prayer can turn a reaction into a wise response.

I stay connected to a small circle of honest friends, the ones I can text when I am wobbly. We tell the truth. We remind each other of perspective. We laugh when we start taking life too seriously.

And then there is music, my secret steering wheel for emotion. It shifts my energy faster than anything else.

At night, I do a quick scan before bed. What emotion led my day? What thought did it feed? What action did it inspire? What reality did that create? It is not about judgment. It is about awareness. Because consistency, not perfection, is what turns a comeback into a lifestyle.

The Everyday Proof

I measure my comeback in small proofs, the quiet evidence that I am still moving forward. The way the gym door feels lighter when I open it myself. The way an audience softens when I smile through a technical hiccup. The way gratitude settles a room. The way awe changes the color of a day.

These are the victories that build a life. The ones no one applauds but matter more than any spotlight ever could.

This is the Comeback Lifestyle. Not a highlight reel but a practiced rhythm. Not a performance but a partnership. Not perfection but presence.

Lead with life-giving emotion. Think with clarity. Act with alignment. Repeat until your days reflect what your heart knows is true.

Your loop becomes your life. Choose your leader well.

Reflection for You

A comeback is not a single decision. It is a rhythm of choices. Emotions you lead with. Thoughts you steward. Actions you repeat. Trust that you will use every piece of your story for something good.

- Which emotion has been leading your days lately, and what reality has it created?
- Which emotion do you want to choose this week, and how will it shape your next thought and action?
- Where can you create a small gap before responding, so wisdom leads instead of urgency?
- Where might God be inviting you to prepare without controlling, rooted like a palm tree and flexible to His timing?

Your comeback does not need to be louder. It needs to be truer, and you get to choose the tone.

CHAPTER 14

Walking in Purpose – Living the Story You Were Created to Tell

The People Who Walk Beside You

Purpose isn't something we discover alone. It's something shaped by the people who walk beside us, the ones who hold us up when life brings us to our knees, who remind us of who we are when we can't quite remember ourselves.

Larry has been that kind of steady for me. His quiet strength and unwavering patience carried me through moments I wasn't sure I could carry myself. From learning how to care for my wounds to helping me navigate prosthetics, he never complained. He simply loved, served, and stayed. I've learned that sometimes faith looks like the person who refuses to leave your side.

My mom lived with us for nine months after I came home, caring for me in ways I can never fully repay. She was my hands when mine couldn't grasp, my cheerleader when progress felt too slow, and the gentle voice reminding me that grace is enough.

And then there's Marian, a friend who became family. After my mom returned home, she took on the task of driving me to therapy appointments week after week, year after year. But she did so much more than drive; she filled those hours with laughter, wisdom, and light. She filmed my progress so I could share it with Team TLT, celebrated every milestone, and showed up at every important event, from the PossAbilities Fashion Show to the I AM Hallway reveal, beaming with pride like it was her own victory too. Marian loved my family, and even our dogs, as if they were her own. Her friendship reminded me daily that healing isn't something you do alone; it's something you're loved through.

Then there are my friends, the ones who showed up with meals, laughter, and late-night talks when I needed both comfort and perspective. The ones who didn't let me sink too low, who offered truth and encouragement in equal measure, and who reminded me that healing happens best in good company.

And my kids—each of them has been a mirror of strength, resilience, and authenticity. They've taught me what it looks like to stay true to who you are, even when life changes everything around you. I've tried to parent with compassion, never muting their voices, but gently guiding them forward when they feel stuck. Watching them grow through all of this reminded me that grace isn't just something we receive; it's something we pass on.

Each relationship has taught me something different about love.
Larry taught me commitment.
My mom taught me compassion.
Marian taught me consistency.
My kids taught me courage, the kind that comes from choosing truth over comfort and hope over fear.
My friends taught me community, that love multiplies when it's shared.

I often think about how the community carried me when I couldn't carry myself. From the nurses who brushed out my tangled hair to the PossAbilities team that gave me new opportunities, I've seen what happens when people choose to show up for one another.

It's easy to look at purpose as something grand and far-reaching, but more often, it's found right here in the people who love you through your process. The ones who remind you that your comeback isn't yours alone.

Because the truth is, we heal in relationships.
We grow in connection.
And we walk in purpose together.

The story God writes through our lives isn't meant to be kept quiet. It's meant to ripple through every relationship, every act of courage, every step of faith, reminding others that hope multiplies when it's shared.

When I look back on the last four years of my life, I know I am a changed person. Tougher. More focused. More at peace with what I can't control. I've learned to say no when I need to and to let time marinate opportunities before I say yes. My faith is stronger. My relationships are deeper. And the vision I hold for my life now feels clearer, given to me by God as a kind of north star. It guides me when I lose sight of what's ahead. It keeps me anchored in who I believe God created me to be. It gives me confidence in my mission and joy in my growth.

This awareness didn't come in one single breakthrough moment. It came through small realizations, through the practice of watching for signs and celebrating growth. My mountaintop moments aren't about standing on a stage or reaching a milestone. They come in the quiet recognition that I am living aligned with what matters most.

Purpose, I've learned, isn't a grand arrival.
It's the daily decision to keep walking.

The Shape of a Life Rebuilt

When you're rebuilding after a major life shift, the world often measures your progress by milestones: walking again, working again, smiling again. But transformation rarely happens in big, cinematic moments. It happens through repetition, through awareness, through the gentle hum of daily life shifting slowly toward something new.

Every small win, a stronger step, a calmer morning, a conversation that once felt impossible, builds a new layer of self-trust. It's these ordinary triumphs that form the structure of a life rebuilt.

And yet, as I look back, I have to be honest.

I'm not at the place yet where I can say I'm grateful for what happened to me. I've heard people say that about their traumas or turning points, that they wouldn't be who they are without them. Maybe one day I'll be able to say the same. But today, I wish it hadn't happened. Not only for me, but for my family.

What I am grateful for is the faithful presence of God and His saving grace. I'm grateful for my family and the joy they bring me, for the close friends who have walked this long road beside me, and for the opportunities that have come because I am an amputee, doors that never would have opened otherwise. I'm grateful for my growth as a woman and the impact I am finally brave enough to make.

Gratitude doesn't always mean approval. It means noticing what's still good and noticing God in it. Choosing to build from there.

That choice, day after day, is where purpose begins.

Purpose Is Movement, Not Milestone

So often, we think purpose belongs to the people doing big things, the entrepreneurs, the authors, the leaders. But purpose isn't confined to titles or platforms. Purpose is motion. It's any moment you step out of comfort and into contribution.

Maybe your story doesn't involve hospitals or hard pivots.

Maybe it's the quieter kind of stuck, the slow settling into routine that feels safe but small.

You might be the professional woman who's been excellent at her job for years but no longer feels alive in it.

Or the mom whose kids are grown and who's wondering what comes next.

Or the woman of faith who's waiting for a sign when God's already placed the invitation right in front of her.

Purpose lives in motion, not mastery. It's not about a new job, a new city, or a big leap. It's about showing up to the life you already have with fresh intention and an open heart.

When you take one small step, volunteering for a cause that stirs your heart, reaching out to a friend who's struggling, starting a project that lights you up, you're already walking in purpose.

The question isn't whether you have a purpose. You do. The question is whether you're willing to live it, right where you are.

The Partnership of Purpose

Purpose isn't something we create, it's something we *receive.* It's given, guided, and grown through partnership with God.

Over these years, I've learned that His plans often unfold slower than our timelines.

Opportunities need time to marinate. Lessons take time to mature. We're asked to stay faithful in the in-between.

That's where trust lives.

Purpose asks for patience. It's the humility to wait for God's "now" instead of pushing our own "not yet." It's staying rooted enough to handle delays, and flexible enough to pivot when a door opens in a direction you didn't expect.

Purpose, like faith, is a long walk of obedience. You can't rush it. You can only stay close to the One leading the way.

And the beautiful thing about walking in purpose is that it doesn't always look grand. Sometimes it looks like saying no when you could have said yes. Sometimes it looks like sitting quietly in gratitude instead of searching for the next mountain to climb.

It's the peace of knowing you're walking with God, not running ahead of Him.

The Everyday Purpose Practice

Purpose isn't found in one big calling. It's practiced in the rhythms of everyday life.

It's the teacher who encourages a student to see her own potential.

The manager who listens with empathy instead of impatience.
The mom who brings laughter back into her home.
The friend who prays when someone else has no words left.
The business owner who leads with integrity, not image.

These are all acts of purpose. Quiet, consistent, transformational.

When I started seeing purpose this way, I stopped measuring my worth by output and started measuring it by presence. Am I showing up with kindness? With excellence? With faith?

That's purpose.

It's not the scale of what you do, it's the spirit in which you do it.

Each day, I ask myself:
What kind of energy am I bringing into this room? Into this relationship? Into this opportunity?

Because impact doesn't always look like a platform. Sometimes it looks like patience. Sometimes it looks like listening. Sometimes it looks like staying.

From Resilience to Radiance

Resilience rebuilt my life. But purpose gave me a reason to shine. Resilience taught me how to endure. Purpose taught me how to expand. Resilience helped me rise from the valley. Purpose helps me walk forward with joy.

The most beautiful transformation isn't just surviving; it's learning to glow again. To find humor where there was heaviness. To find grace where there was grief. To find peace in progress.

That's what I want for every woman who reads this book, to remember that she doesn't have to stay stuck. Her story may not look like mine, but her purpose is just as powerful.

You might be in a chapter that feels uncertain. You might be rebuilding your confidence, your relationships, or your sense of identity. But you're not behind; you're growing.

The comeback life is available to anyone willing to live awake, to stop waiting for clarity and start walking toward it.

Living Legacy – What We Leave in Motion

There's a quiet moment that comes when you realize your story has started to ripple. You notice it in an email from a stranger who felt seen, in a conversation that brings comfort to someone who's struggling, or in the way your family looks at you with pride after everything you've endured.

That's legacy.

It's not what we leave behind when we're gone, it's what we set in motion while we're still here.

Every act of courage, every honest word, every story told in love adds light to someone else's path.

I used to think my story was about loss.

Now I see it's about *life.*

Because God wastes nothing. Every broken piece can become a building block in someone else's healing.

When we walk in purpose, we become part of something much bigger than ourselves. We become carriers of grace in motion.

Every time I step onto a stage now, sharing my story as a keynote speaker or connecting with women online at *ToughLikeTammy.com*, I'm reminded that purpose multiplies when it's shared.

Reflection for You

Purpose doesn't wait for the perfect moment, it's discovered in the steps you're already taking.

- Where do you sense God calling you to walk more boldly right now?

- What small daily act could create ripple effects of good in your world?
- How might you reframe "stuck" as an invitation to grow?
- What would it look like to trust that your purpose doesn't have to be perfect to be powerful?
- Who might be waiting for the light only you can bring?

Your purpose isn't waiting on someday.
It's waiting on your *yes*.

Prayer

Father God,

Thank You for walking with us through every season, the storms, the stillness, and the stretch.
Thank You for Your grace that steadies our steps when we can't see the road ahead.

We ask for courage to live our stories out loud, for wisdom to discern what truly matters, and for faith to follow Your timing instead of forcing our own.

Remind us that purpose isn't a destination but a daily partnership with You, one that transforms our hearts and brightens the world around us.

As we go forward, let our lives be reflections of Your goodness and grace.

May we walk in confidence, compassion, and gratitude, trusting that You will continue to use every piece of our story for something good.

In Jesus Name, Amen.

A Letter from Tammy

Dear friend,

If you've made it here, thank you. Thank you for letting my story meet you where you are, and for allowing these pages to speak to the part of you that's still learning, still growing, still rising.

Writing this book has been one of the most humbling and healing experiences of my life. Not because it ties everything up neatly, life rarely does, but because it's a reminder that transformation isn't a destination. It's a lifelong movement. The courage to show up, to tell the truth, to take one small step forward even when the way isn't clear, that's what changes everything.

If there's one thing I want you to take from these pages, it's this: you are not behind. You are in motion. You are already being refined, already discovering new strength, already moving toward something good.

Maybe your comeback looks different than mine. Maybe it's quieter, less public, more internal. Maybe you're rebuilding your confidence after disappointment, or simply trying to rediscover joy after a long season of holding it together. Whatever your chapter looks like, know this: God is still writing. And He writes the best stories.

Your past does not disqualify you. Your pauses do not define you. And your purpose is not lost; it's waiting for you to say yes.

When I think about what comes next, for both of us, I picture a steady rhythm. Not a sprint. Not a climb. Just one faithful movement at a time.

That's where resilience becomes strength, and strength becomes confidence. That's where life begins to expand again.

You don't have to see the whole path to move forward. You just have to trust that you were made for this moment.

So, wherever you are as you close this book, take a deep breath.
Look at how far you've come.
And remember: this isn't the end of your story, it's a new beginning.

If these words have met you in a meaningful way, I'd love to stay connected with you.

Join me on Instagram @toughliketammy for daily encouragement and real-life reflections, or visit my website ToughLikeTammy.com for speaking updates, resources, and ways we can keep growing together.

More than anything, I want you to know this:
Thank you for letting me be a small part of your journey.
I believe in you, your strength, your story, and your ability to rise again.

And if you're holding this book in your hands, you've already seen the tulip on its cover. To me, it's more than just a flower, it's a reflection of grace, resilience, and my heritage. Tulips stand tall in their simplicity, returning year after year with quiet confidence. They remind me that beauty doesn't need to strive or prove; it just blooms in its time. That's what I hope this story whispers to you: that elegance and strength can coexist, that renewal can be both simple and profound, and that even after the hardest winters, new life is still possible.

Keep moving. The world needs your light.

With love and gratitude,
Tammy Gibson

Acknowledgments

To my husband, Larry, there aren't enough words to express my gratitude for you. I know these years haven't been easy. Thank you for your love, for being my problem-solver, and for handling every detail of my care with patience and grace. You've been my steady through it all, and I love you deeply.

To our children, Nick and Montana, thank you for bringing so much joy and purpose into my life. You remind me every day why I keep moving forward. To Lesley, Rob, and Grayson, thank you for being constant sources of encouragement and joy.

To my mom and dad, thank you for your endless prayers, steady faith, and love that continues to anchor me.

To Erica, Ameris, Jacqueline, Rebecca, Mary, and Susie, thank you for the laughter, the lunch dates, the honest conversations, and the kind of friendship that makes life brighter.

To Marian, thank you for your friendship and the countless ways you showed up. Your generosity and kindness sustained me on many of the hardest days.

To Team TLT, thank you for your prayers, encouragement, and unwavering support through every season of this journey. You've been my community of hope and strength, and I'm forever grateful.

To my therapists and O&P team, thank you for your outstanding care, skill, and steady presence through every stage of my recovery.

Each of you has walked this journey in a completely different way, and I pray you are healing too. Your strength, your resilience, and your ability to adapt remind me daily just how extraordinary you are.

And most of all, to God, thank you for the miracle of my life. Every page, every lesson, every breath is proof of Your grace.

About the Author

Tammy Gibson is a speaker, writer, and advocate for resilience whose story of survival and faith has inspired audiences around the world. After a life-threatening illness led to the amputation of her right leg and years of recovery, Tammy discovered that her greatest comeback wasn't just physical; it was spiritual, emotional, and deeply personal.

Today, she helps others find strength, confidence, and purpose in their own stories. Through her speaking engagements, digital resources, and her platform Tough Like Tammy, she empowers women and professionals alike to turn their challenges into catalysts for growth and leadership.

Tammy's message blends faith, humor, and honesty, reminding us that life's most powerful transformations often begin in the moments we least expect. Her signature approach, what she calls *The Comeback Edit*, guides others in rewriting the stories they tell themselves so they can live with clarity, courage, and joy.

She lives in Redlands, California, with her husband, Larry, and their family, where she continues to embrace the beautiful, messy, joy-filled rhythm of life after loss and proof that even in hardship, grace always has the final word.

Connect with Tammy at **ToughLikeTammy.com** or on Instagram **@ToughLikeTammy** for encouragement, resources, and updates on her latest speaking events.

The Comeback Companion

This section gathers every reflection prompt, key quote, and Scripture from The Comeback Edit.

Use it as your personal guide for journalling, group discussions, or moments of quiet reflection.

Quotes To Remember

- Survival isn't the finish line. It's the invitation to begin again with a deeper kind of strength.
- The ticking clock is my ally, not my enemy.
- The biggest freedom you can give yourself is to stop making excuses, placing blame, or being the victim. Take ownership in every area of your life.
- Embrace your life pivots, for within them lies the power to transform, to rise, and to thrive.
- Grace doesn't remove the challenge; it redefines it.
- Peace isn't passive, it's power under control.
- Your loop becomes your life. Choose your leader well.
- You don't have to see the whole path to move forward.

Scriptures That Anchored My Journey

- Psalm 23:4 NIV Even though I walk through the darkest valley, I will fear no evil, for you are with me; your rod and your staff, they comfort me.

- Philippians 4:13 NIV I can do all things through Christ who gives me strength.
- 2 Corinthians 12:9 NIV My grace is sufficient for you, for my power is made perfect in weakness.
- Romans 8:28 NIV And we know that in all things God works for the good of those who love him, who have been called according to his purpose.
- Psalm 46:5 NIV God is within her, she will not fall; God will help her at break of day.
- Ephesians 3:20 NIV Now to him who is able to do immeasurably more than all we ask or imagine, according to his power that is at work within us.
- Romans 15:13 May the God of hope fill you with all joy and peace as you trust in Him, so that you may overflow with hope by the power of the Holy Spirit.

Reflections For Your Comeback

Chapter 1: The Pivot I Never Saw Coming

- What was the pivot you never saw coming?
- How did it shift the way you saw yourself or your future?
- Looking back, where can you see God's presence woven in, even if you did not recognize it at the time?

Chapter 2: Life or Limb

- What have you had to release in order to live?
- How has the loss of a person, role, or identity, reshaped your understanding of purpose?
- What does choosing life look like for you right now?

Chapter 3: When the Tides Turn

- Where in your life have you quietly accepted "this is just the way it is"?
- What's one small step you could take this week toward healing, growth, or change?
- How might faith and action together open space for God to rewrite your story?

Chapter 4: Coming Home to a Stranger

- Have you ever found yourself in a season where you didn't recognize the woman in the mirror?
- What parts of your identity have you been clinging to that no longer fit?

- How might God be inviting you to release the old and step into who you are becoming now?

Chapter 5: Learning to Stand Again

- What "rehab season" are you in right now, physically, emotionally, or spiritually?
- Where are you pressuring yourself to go faster than your healing allows?
- How could you celebrate progress today, even if it feels small?

Chapter 6: The Identity Comeback

- Where in your story are you learning to see yourself with new eyes?
- What pieces of your identity have shifted, and how might God be using that shift to shape something beautiful?
- Can you bless who you were, honor who you are, and trust who you are becoming?

Chapter 7: Called to Rise

- What truth might you share that could give someone else courage?
- Where could you turn your own lessons into light for others?
- What if your story, the one you have been hesitant to tell, is the very thing God intends to use?

Chapter 8: Obedience in Action

- Where is God asking you to step out of comfort and into calling?
- What opportunities might already be waiting for your "yes"?

- What part of your story is ready to be used for good?

Chapter 9: Building the Mission

- Where might you be overcomplicating what God is asking you to do?
- What pressure could you release to make space for peace?
- What golden thread has been woven through your own story all along?

Chapter 10: The Space Between Strength and Surrender

- What has God actually asked me to carry today?
- Where am I striving from fear instead of flowing from faith?
- What would it look like to trust His timing, even if it means slowing down?

Chapter 11: The Comeback Edit – Rewriting the Story You Tell Yourself

- Where do you sense it's time to pause before you press forward?
- What truth have you been avoiding that might actually set you free?
- Which habits or expectations could you refine to create more space for peace and progress?
- How might you rebuild your days, not to prove you're back, but to honor the woman you've become?

Chapter 12: Grace Under Pressure

- Where do you feel pressure showing up in your life right now?

- What expectation could you release to create more space for grace?
- Who has been a vessel of grace for you lately and how can you extend that same kindness to yourself?
- What does living with grace under pressure look like for you today, not in theory but in action?

Chapter 13: The Comeback Lifestyle – Living Within the Reality Loop

- Which emotion has been leading your days lately, and what reality has it created?
- Which emotion do you want to choose this week, and how will it shape your next thought and action?
- Where can you create a small gap before responding, so wisdom leads instead of urgency?
- Where might God be inviting you to prepare without controlling, rooted like a palm tree and flexible to His timing?

Chapter 14: Walking in Purpose – Living the Story You Were Created to Tell

- Where do you sense God calling you to walk more boldly right now?
- What small daily act could create ripple effects of good in your world?
- How might you reframe "stuck" as an invitation to grow?
- What would it look like to trust that your purpose doesn't have to be perfect to be powerful?
- Who might be waiting for the light only you can bring?

◆ ◆ ◆

Because your story matters...and it's still being written.

With love and resilience,
Tammy

Your Next Edit Begins Here

If something in these pages stirred you, pause here for a moment. That response matters.

The Comeback Edit: Life Beyond Survival Mode was never meant to be the end of the conversation. It's an invitation to continue the work in the community, where stories are honored, faith is centered, and women are encouraged to step forward with clarity and courage.

You've done hard things. Now let's do big things.

If you're part of a women's group, organization, church, or leadership community, I would be honored to come and speak at your event. Whether it's a retreat, conference, luncheon, or intimate gathering, I love creating spaces where women can reflect, reconnect, and move beyond survival mode together.

Here's how to continue:

- **Visit ToughLikeTammy.com** to explore speaking topics, event experiences, and resources designed for women navigating meaningful life transitions.
- **Join my email community** for faith-rooted encouragement, reflection prompts, and updates on upcoming events and offerings.
- **Join me on Instagram** at **@toughliketammy**, where I share encouragement, behind-the-scenes moments, and reminders that your story still matters.

- **Reach out directly** if you're planning a women's event and feel this message aligns with your community. I'd be honored to partner with you.

You don't need to rush. But you don't need to do this alone.

What you've survived matters.
What you choose next matters just as much.

If this book met you in a tender or courageous place, consider this your invitation to bring the conversation beyond the page.

Your story is still unfolding.
And you're allowed to shape what comes next.

www.ingramcontent.com/pod-product-compliance
Lightning Source LLC
Chambersburg PA
CBHW051544050726
47595CB00002B/626